Beyond The Pitch Deck

How To Raise Startup Capital

About the Author

Australian Local Search had no customers yet. Murray Longe was already in the room with Yahoo!, pitching hard enough to walk out with a signed launch partnership. Eighteen months later, with the business running, he closed a second partnership with Google. That sequence, and everything it took to make both happen, is the foundation of this book.

Murray co-founded Australian Local Search, which launched in Australia with Yahoo! and later partnered with Google, before being acquired by News Limited and becoming TrueLocal.com.au. He subsequently co-founded YourLocal.ie in Ireland. Both companies required him to raise venture capital and close deals that most founders never attempt. He learned that getting funded has less to do with the deck and more to do with the work done before anyone opens it.

Beyond the Pitch Deck is his fourth book in the Startup Success Series, following *Find Problems Worth Solving*, *Beyond the Minimum Viable Product*, and *Scale Without Breaking*. It is his sixth published book. The series gives founders a practical guide to each stage of building a startup, drawn from real experience rather than theory.

Murray writes for founders doing the actual work. This book is their guide to raising startup capital.

The Startup Success Series Book 4

Beyond The Pitch Deck

How To Raise Startup Capital

Murray Longe

WHITMAN
CROSS

Published by Whitman Cross Publishing, Melbourne, Australia.

First edition 2026

ISBN 978-1-7645438-2-8 (ebook)
ISBN 978-1-7645438-3-5 (paperback)

NATIONAL LIBRARY OF AUSTRALIA

A catalogue record for this book is available from the National Library of Australia

Disclaimer

The information in this book represents the author's views as of the date of publication. It is for general informational purposes only and is not intended as professional, legal, financial, or business advice. Because circumstances and regulations change, the author reserves the right to revise his views in light of new conditions. Readers should consider their own personal circumstances and consult with qualified professionals before taking any action based on the information in this book. While every effort has been made to ensure the accuracy and completeness of the information, the author and publisher assume no responsibility for any errors, omissions, or inaccuracies. Use of the information is at the reader's own risk.

For more information, visit whitmancross.com

WHITMAN CROSS

Also by Murray Longe

How To Start Your Start-Up:
The 10 Key Steps To Get From Idea To Investment

Project Management for Startups:
Simple Tools and Templates to Launch, Lead, and Thrive

The Startup Success Series

\#1 *Find Problems Worth Solving:*
How to Validate Your Startup Idea

\#2 *Beyond The Minimum Viable Product:*
Build Products Customers Really Want

\#3 *Scale Without Breaking:*
How to Grow Your Startup Without Losing What Made It Work

\#4 *Beyond The Pitch Deck:*
How to Raise Startup Capital

Search All "Murray Longe"

in your amazon store

For every founder who has sat across the table from someone who said no.
And for everyone who went back anyway.

Raising capital is tough. It's one of the most personally testing things you'll do as a founder. The rejections pile up. The silence after a pitch you thought went well is brutal. There are days when the whole idea feels foolish.

It is not foolish. It is just hard.

Every founder who has ever closed a funding round has been in the same spot you're in now. They faced the same rejections. They felt the same doubt. They kept going, and so can you.

This book is written for you.

Murray Longe
March 2026

CONTENTS

CONTENTS

CONTENTS

INTRODUCTION
The Most Expensive Mistake You'll Make

Most founders who seek funding don't fail because their business isn't good enough.

They fail because they walked into the process without understanding what they were actually doing.

They didn't know which type of capital suited their situation. They pitched the wrong investors in the wrong order. They signed terms they didn't fully understand. They took money from someone whose expectations were fundamentally misaligned with their own. And then, when the relationship became difficult, they had no framework for navigating it.

This book exists because that pattern is entirely preventable.

Funding is among the most important decisions a founder makes. Not because the money itself matters, but because the terms you agree to and the people you take it from shape everything that follows. The investor on your cap table can affect your timeline, your strategic options, your culture, and sometimes your ongoing role in the company you've built. Get that decision right and the capital can accelerate everything. Get it wrong and it can create a pressure that never fully eases.

And yet, many founders go into the process with minimal preparation for the decisions that truly matter.

They read pitch deck guides and practise their elevator pitch. They study how to answer investor questions. They optimise for getting a yes. What they rarely do is step back and ask whether they should be raising at all, from whom, on what terms, and what they plan to do with the relationship once the capital arrives.

This book covers all of it.

Who This Book Is For

You are a founder, or someone seriously thinking about becoming one, who has reached a point where external funding is available. You have some level of traction: early income, a product that resonates with genuine customers, or a validated problem with a credible plan to fix it. You are not at the very start, still searching for a problem worth solving. That stage is behind you. Now, you're focusing on what's next.

Maybe you have already started conversations with investors and found them confusing or unclear. Maybe you haven't started yet and want to understand what you're getting into before you do. Perhaps you've raised a small round and are trying to work out how to manage the relationship and plan for the next one.

Wherever you are in that range, this book starts where you are and takes you through the full journey: from deciding whether to raise, to choosing the right type of capital, to understanding what you sign, to managing investors well enough that they become your greatest asset in every subsequent raise.

What This Book Is Not

This isn't a guide to writing a pitch deck, though Chapter 4 explains what makes a pitch work and why. It's not a legal manual, though Chapters 7 and 8 provide the understanding needed to read a term sheet properly before your lawyer summarises it. It's not a book solely about venture capital, though VC is covered in depth. It covers the full range of funding options because choosing between them is the decision most other books skip entirely.

It is also not written from the investor's perspective, though understanding how investors think runs through every chapter. It is written for founders. Your interests are the ones this book is designed to protect.

Where This Book Fits in the Series

This is the fourth book in the Startup Success Series. The first three covered finding a problem worth solving, building a product your customers genuinely want, and scaling without breaking what you built.

This book sits alongside those books as a parallel track rather than a strict next step. Not every founder who validates a problem and develops a product needs external capital. Some of the most successful businesses covered in this series grew entirely on revenue. But for founders who reach a point where external capital could genuinely accelerate what they're building, and who want to approach that decision with clarity rather than reflex, this is the book for that moment.

A Word on What Comes After

Raising capital is not the destination. Every founder who has been through the process will tell you the same thing: the raise itself is the easy part compared to what follows. The relationship with your investors, the discipline required to deploy capital well, the pressure of operating with other people's money and other people's expectations, and the work of setting up the next raise while running the current business: those are the real tests.

This book covers all of it, not just the pitch and the close. The chapters on managing investors, navigating tough moments, and organising the next raise are some of the most important because they address parts most fundraising guides completely overlook.

The goal by the time you finish is simple. You should have a clear understanding of the entire funding process so that you can make every decision deliberately, rather than by default. This understanding is more valuable than any pitch deck template or term sheet guide. It makes the difference between a founder who raises capital and one who effectively uses it.

Let's start with the question most people skip.

1

Are You Actually Ready?

Around 2004–2005, Evan Williams was building a podcasting startup called Odeo. He had already co-created Blogger, sold it to Google, and had the kind of founder credibility that gets meetings. Investors listened, and Odeo secured backing, but when Apple integrated podcasting into iTunes, Odeo's prospects dimmed and growth stalled.

What followed is now startup history. Recognising that the product wasn't working, Williams and his team ran internal hack-style sessions to explore new ideas. One of those sessions surfaced Jack Dorsey's simple concept for sharing short status updates, which evolved into Twitter. As Twitter began to show real user traction, raising money for it became far easier than it had been for Odeo, and investors were invited back in at a higher valuation.

The lesson Williams drew from Odeo's failure was straightforward: conviction alone isn't proof. Even a convincing founder with a solid track record couldn't substitute for a product that the market genuinely responded to. When the evidence was lacking, the fundraising reflected that. When the evidence was present, everything shifted.

This happens every week in meeting rooms and coffee shops across the startup scene. A founder gets a warm introduction to an investor. They've spent three weekends fine-tuning their pitch deck. The meeting lasts 45 minutes. The investor is polite, asks decent questions, and says they'll be in touch. They never are. The founder follows up twice. The response is a polite pass with no useful feedback.

What went wrong? Often, nothing was wrong with the pitch itself. The founder simply wasn't ready to be raising funds, and the investor knew it within the first ten minutes.

This happens all the time. It's one of the most costly mistakes a founder can make, not because a single meeting is expensive, but because the startup investing community is smaller than it appears. Investors talk. Fund partners share notes with each other. An angel in your city knows the seed fund partners. The seed fund partners know the Series A investors. When you pitch before you're ready, you don't just lose one meeting. You can close a door you'll want open in twelve months when you actually are ready.

The good news is that "ready" is not a feeling. It's not confidence, and it's not having a perfect product or a polished deck. It is a set of specific signals that investors look for at each stage of the funding process. Know the signals. Have the signals. Then raise.

What Investors Are Actually Looking For

A lot of first-time founders assume that investors evaluate ideas. Some do, particularly very early angels who back founders on instinct and a strong concept. But most investors are evaluating evidence. They want to see proof that something real is happening before they write a check.

The specific proof they need depends entirely on the stage of funding you're seeking. Seed investors and Series A investors are asking very different questions, and the bar between them is much higher than most founders expect.

At seed Stage, investors are backing your early conviction and your evidence of a real problem. You don't need scale. You need a signal. That signal might come from a working prototype with genuine user engagement, from early paying customers who chose you without being pushed, from a clear and specific problem that a definable group of people urgently wants solved, or from a founding team whose backgrounds make them unusually well-suited to win in this space.

The keyword here is "genuine." Ten users who signed up because you're their friend is not a signal. Five customers who pay you every month because your product saves them real money or time, that's a signal.

At Series A, the conversation changes entirely. Series A investors are not betting on a concept or a founding team's potential. They are buying into a business that has already found its footing. They want to see revenue growing at a meaningful rate, a clear and repeatable process for bringing in new customers, unit economics that suggest the business can be profitable at scale, and a management team capable of running something bigger than what exists today.

If you go to a Series A investor with seed-stage evidence, you will not get funded. You will get a polite suggestion to come back in 12 to 18 months. That is the kindest outcome. Less kind investors will pass without giving you any useful direction at all.

The chart below outlines the key signals investors look for at each stage. These aren't guarantees. Investing is never purely formulaic, and strong teams with compelling stories sometimes raise funds with less. But these are the benchmarks you should be able to demonstrate before you walk into a meeting.

The Funding Readiness Signal Map

A two-column comparison showing the key signals required at seed vs Series A.

Signal	Seed Stage	Series A
Product	Working prototype or early version	Stable product with strong retention
Customers	Early adopters showing genuine demand	Paying customers with growing base
Revenue	Not required, but pre-sales or letters of intent help	Typically $500K-$2M ARR with clear growth trajectory
Growth	Early evidence of demand	Consistent month-on-month revenue growth (15-20%+ MoM or 2-3x YoY)
Unit Economics	You have a rough estimate of customer costs and returns and understand the direction even if the numbers aren't precise	Customer acquisition cost and lifetime value clearly defined and improving
Team	Founders with relevant domain knowledge	Leadership team with functional depth
Market	Large, clearly defined, and accessible	Validated through actual customer data
What you need to explain	Why this problem matters and why you can solve it	Why your business will dominate this market

Note: These are directional benchmarks, not strict requirements. Investors vary in their thresholds. The most successful rounds surpass these benchmarks.

The Timing Trap

Understanding what investors look for is only half the equation. The other half is knowing when to show them. Most founders get this wrong in the same direction.

Most founders pitch too early. Some pitch too late, which is its own problem, but the far more common mistake is going to market before the evidence is there.

There are three different versions of this trap.

The first is pitching on vision alone. Some founders have a compelling idea, strong conviction, and genuine energy. They pitch before they have customers, a product, or data. A small number of superstar founders in demonstrably large markets raise this way. Their success creates the impression it's a viable general strategy. It isn't. For every pre-product raise that works, there are dozens of founders who wasted months of their most important early time trying to raise on a pitch that wasn't ready.

The second, and most common, is pitching with soft traction. The founder has something: a few customers, some encouraging feedback, and early product usage. The evidence isn't crisp enough to be compelling and the founder can't articulate it in a way that creates investor confidence. They get meetings but can't close them.

The third is the easiest to fix. **Strong traction but a weak story.** The founder actually has the evidence to raise funds. They simply present it in a way that buries the signal under product details and feature lists. They are ready to raise. Their pitch doesn't communicate that. This problem can be solved with better preparation.

The Reputation Cost

Investors keep notes. They share them with partners at their fund and with investors at other funds they know and trust. If you pitch a seed fund when you're not ready, the fund might pass this week, but they will also remember what stage you were at and what evidence you had.

This matters more than most founders realise because investor networks are tightly connected. A typical seed fund partner in any major startup market knows dozens of other active investors personally. They share deal flow, co-invest regularly, and talk informally about founders they've met. When a Series A fund is evaluating your company, one of the first calls they often make is to investors who have seen you before, including those who passed. What these investors say, and how they remember the stage you first pitched, shapes the conversation even before they open your deck.

This doesn't mean you should never talk to investors before you're ready to raise funds. Relationship-building chats are different from fundraising pitches, and savvy founders treat them that way. A coffee catch-up where you're asking for perspective, not capital, does not carry the same stakes as a formal pitch. But the moment you put a deck in front of someone and ask for money, you're pitching. Make sure you're prepared when that happens.

Your Optimism Is Working Against You Here

The toughest part of this chapter is the honesty it demands. Founders are inherently optimists by nature. They have to be. Building a company requires believing in a future that hasn't happened yet.

But the same optimism that makes founders resilient can also make them terrible at accurately assessing their own readiness. "We're almost there" is not a funding stage. "We have some great early feedback" is not traction data.

The readiness checklist below aims to cut through the optimism and provide you with a clear, evidence-based assessment of where you stand. Answer each question based on what you can demonstrate to a skeptical stranger, not based on what you believe to be true or what you expect will be true in three months.

Readiness Checklist: Before You Start the Process

Problem and Market

- Can you describe the problem in one sentence that a non-expert immediately understands?
- Can you name at least five specific people or companies who have this problem and are actively looking for a solution?
- Can you explain why this market is large enough to support a real business?

Product and Traction

- Do you have something a customer can use today?
- Have customers used it without you guiding them through every step?
- Do any customers come back, and can you show that data?

Revenue and Unit Economics (critical for Series A, directional for seed)

- If you have revenue, can you show consistent growth over at least six months?
- Do you know what it costs you, in total sales and marketing spend, to bring in one new customer?
- Do you know how much revenue a typical customer generates before they stop buying from you?

Team

- Can you explain why this team is the best to solve this problem?
- Is there a clear gap in the founding team that you need to fill, and do you know what it is?

Funding Mechanics

- Do you know how much you need to raise and what you'll spend it on?
- Can you explain what milestone the capital will get you to?
- Do you know what stage of funding is appropriate for where you are right now?

If you can answer every question above with clear, specific, evidence-backed answers, you're very likely ready to start the process. If several answers are vague or rely on future assumptions, consider that useful information. The work to do is in the building, not the pitching.

The chapters that follow assume you've worked through this checklist and made an honest decision. If you need more time to build before you raise, that's not a failure. That's good judgment. The best raises are the ones that close quickly because the evidence was already there before the first meeting started.

Chapter 2 takes you a step back: before planning the raise, you need to decide whether raising funds is the right path for your business at all.

2

Should You Raise at All?

Every piece of advice about raising capital assumes you've already decided to go ahead. The pitch deck guides, the term sheet explanations, the warm introduction playbooks: all of it starts after the decision has been made.

That's a problem. Because for many founders, the decision itself is the most important one they'll make in the early stages of their company, and they often make it by default rather than through deliberate planning.

"I'm building a startup, so I need to raise." That's not a decision. That's a reflex.

This chapter is here to turn the reflex into a conscious choice. External capital is a genuine tool that can help the right business at the right time. It is also a constraint, an obligation, and a lasting change to what you're building. Both of these are true, and you need to understand each before you go looking for it.

What Capital Actually Costs

When founders consider the cost of raising funds, they often think about equity. They understand they'll give up a percentage of the company. But equity dilution is only the most obvious aspect of what you're trading.

Here's what else changes when you bring in external capital.

Your timeline is no longer your own. Investors have their own timelines. An angel investor backing your seed round expects to see an outcome, a return, an exit, or a significant raise within a reasonable period. An institutional fund has a set lifespan, usually ten years, and must return capital to its own investors within that time. If you plan to build for fifteen years, you are fundamentally misaligned with most of the investors who will back you.

Major decisions require agreement. Depending on the terms you sign, some decisions will require investor approval, such as hiring senior executives, making acquisitions, raising more capital, and sometimes changing the product direction. The exact details depend entirely on what you negotiate. But the core principle holds: once someone else owns a piece of your company, they have a say in how it is run.

You now have a fiduciary duty. This is the one founders often overlook. When you accept someone's money to build a business, you are legally and ethically required to act in the best interests of the company and its shareholders. That is a different operating mode from creating something solely because you believe in it.

None of this makes external capital a bad choice. For many businesses, it is the right choice, possibly the only choice that gives the company a chance to reach its potential. But it should be a conscious decision, made with a clear understanding of what you're gaining and what you're giving up.

The Alternatives Are Real

One of the most persistent myths in the startup world is that serious companies raise venture capital. The suggestion is that founders who don't secure funding are either not ambitious enough or not good enough to attract investment.

That is not true. Some of the most successful business-builders in the world have never taken a cent of external equity.

Basecamp, the project management software company, has been profitable and privately owned for over two decades. Its founders have written extensively about the choice to stay small and stay in control. Mailchimp built to over $800 million in annual revenue before its eventual acquisition, entirely without venture capital. These are not marginal examples. They are proof that the ambition to build something great does not require giving away the equity to do it.

There are several genuine alternatives to equity funding, and each suits different situations.

Bootstrapping means building on revenue. You fund growth from what the business earns. This approach is slower than burning investor capital, but it forces discipline, keeps you aligned with your customers rather than your investors, and keeps you in control. It works best for businesses that can generate revenue quickly and do not need significant upfront infrastructure or technology investments.

Revenue-based financing is a relatively new option that has seen substantial growth. A lender provides capital in return for a percentage of future monthly revenue until a fixed multiple of the original investment is repaid. No equity is surrendered. The cost is the revenue share, which can be significant, but the founder keeps full ownership. This works well for businesses with predictable and growing revenue, typically $200,000 to $500,000 annually or more. Clearco and Lighter Capital are among the most well-known providers worldwide. In Australia, providers like Choco Up and various fintech lenders have increased access to this model.

Government grants are the least used option on this list. Non-dilutive capital, meaning capital that requires no equity and creates no debt, is available to founders in sectors including deep tech, biotech, clean energy, and advanced manufacturing. In Australia, the R&D Tax Incentive and Accelerating Commercialisation program have provided significant capital to qualifying businesses. The US and UK have similar programs. The trade-off is time: applications are detailed, reporting requirements are real, and the capital often takes time to arrive. But for founders in qualifying sectors, it offers some of the best capital available. The cost is patience, not ownership.

Strategic partnerships are more accessible than most founders realise. A corporate partner, a supplier, a distributor, or a large potential customer may be willing to fund development in exchange for preferred access, exclusivity, or co-development rights. This is not charity. It is a commercial arrangement where both parties see value. The founder gets capital without giving up equity. The partner gets early access to something they believe will be useful to them. Finding the right corporate partner takes relationship-building and takes time, but the terms are often more favourable than any financial investor would offer.

Customer pre-payment is the simplest option of all, and the one most founders overlook entirely. If a customer wants your solution badly enough, they may pay for it before it is fully built. Dropbox used early sign-ups and committed waiting-list demand to validate the product and generate revenue before the full version was available. That committed demand reduced the risk of building and meant the company entered its first institutional conversations with evidence of real appetite rather than an assumption of it. If your customers have an urgent enough problem, asking them to pay early is not a strange request. It is a test of how much they actually need what you are building.

The comparison on the following page maps each path against the variables that matter most when making this choice.

Funding Path Comparison

A comparison matrix across five funding paths, evaluated on six dimensions:

	Boot-strapping	Revenue-Based Financing	Grants	Strategic Partnership	Angel/ seed	Series A
Equity given up	None	None	None	Sometimes small	10-25%	20-30%
Control retained	Full	Full	Full	Mostly	Partial	Partial
Speed to capital	Slow	Medium	Slow	Variable	Medium	Slow
Revenue required	Yes	Yes ($200K+)	No	No	No	Yes ($500K+)
Reporting obligations	None	Monthly	Significant	Variable	Investor updates	Board / formal
Best suited for	Sustainable growth business	Revenue-positive, scalable	Deep tech, research, IP	Business with corporate appeal	High-growth, pre-revenue to early revenue	Proven, fast-growing business

Unit economics refers to the revenue and costs generated by a single customer. This concept is covered in depth in Chapter 4.

The Question You Need to Answer First

The table above shows you the options. What it cannot show you is which one fits what you actually want to build. That requires answering a harder question first, one that sits underneath nearly every significant decision a founder makes.

Do you want to build a large company that generates wealth, or do you want to build and run a company you control?

Most founders say "both." And that is understandable, because at the very beginning, both options seem equally possible. But data collected from thousands of startups consistently shows that these two goals often demand different decisions at almost every crossroads. The co-founder you select, the investors you bring on, the executives you hire, and the ownership structure, known as the cap table, that you establish: each one of these choices either moves you towards scale or towards maintaining control. You rarely get both fully.

Think about what each path actually means in practice. On the control path, you might build a $10 million business that generates $2 million in annual profit, pay yourself well throughout, and own it entirely when you decide to sell. On the wealth-maximising path, you might raise $20 million across four rounds, dilute down to 8% ownership, and sell for $200 million. Your 8% is worth $16 million at exit. Both are excellent outcomes. They require completely different decisions along the way, and they feel completely different to live through. Know which one you're aiming for before choosing your funding path.

This isn't about ambition. External capital, especially venture capital, pushes you strongly toward wealth creation. That's intentional. Investors aren't supporting you just to let you pursue what you love. They're backing you so the company grows big enough to return their investment. If that matches what you want, venture capital can be a great boost. If not, it can turn your own business into a constant source of pressure.

When the Path Isn't Agreed

In 1999, Jason Fried and his co-founders started a web design firm in Chicago called 37signals. About five years later, they built a simple project-management tool to keep their own client work on track and decided to release it to the public. That internal tool became Basecamp.

At the time, the conventional playbook for a software product that was catching on was clear: raise venture capital, hire fast, and grab as much of the market as you could before someone else did. Investors were interested. The opportunity was real.

Fried and his co-founder, David Heinemeier Hansson, said no to the usual growth script. They kept the team small, ran the business profitably from early on, and treated growth as a byproduct of making something genuinely useful rather than a target to be maximized. In 2006 they did accept a minority personal investment from Jeff Bezos, via his firm Bezos Expeditions, but the company stayed largely self-funded, founder-controlled, and profitable. Years later, they even renamed the company after its flagship product, Basecamp.

By the mid-2010s, Basecamp was adding thousands of new clients every week and generating tens of millions of dollars in annual revenue, all with a staff of only a few dozen people. Over the years, more than 20 million people have used Basecamp, and the company has continued to make money without ever taking institutional venture capital. Fried and Hansson have written and spoken at length about this choice in books like *Rework,* and *It Doesn't Have to Be Crazy at Work*, arguing that the pressure to grow at all costs inevitably changes what you build, how you treat your customers, and what your company becomes—and they didn't want to make that trade.

Jan Koum grew up in poverty in Ukraine and moved to the United States as a teenager. When he co-founded WhatsApp in 2009, he set out to build a communication tool that could serve hundreds of millions of people worldwide. Reaching that kind of global scale required capital he didn't have, so WhatsApp raised outside funding, and each round diluted his ownership. He accepted that because the mission required scale, and scale required capital. By early 2014, WhatsApp had grown to over 400 million monthly active users and was handling tens of billions of messages a day, making it one of the largest messaging networks on the planet. When Facebook agreed to acquire WhatsApp in 2014 in a deal valued at about 19 billion dollars, Koum's stake had been significantly diluted from his founding position, but it was still worth several billion dollars on its own. More importantly for him, he had built exactly the kind of global communication network he set out to create.

Neither Fried nor Koum made the wrong decision. They made different choices, each suited to what they were actually trying to achieve. That alignment is what this chapter aims for you to discover.

Questions to Answer Before You Decide

Work through these before you move on to the rest of this book.

On your goals. What does a good personal outcome look like for you in ten years? Is it owning the company, earning a financial return from a sale, generating ongoing income, or building something that matters at scale? Be specific.

On your business. Does your business need a lot of capital to reach its potential, or can it get there on revenue alone? Is there a specific window of time in your market that you'll miss if you don't grow quickly? Or is the market growing steadily and a disciplined pace is fine?

On your personality. How do you feel about having investors to report to? Are you comfortable with your major decisions being subject to other people's input? Do you want an investor group that can challenge your thinking, or does that feel like a constraint you'll resent?

On your alternatives. Have you seriously explored the non-equity paths? Have you calculated what revenue-based financing would cost compared to diluting by 20% at your current valuation? Have you looked at what grants you might qualify for?

There are no right answers. There are only honest ones.

If you work through these questions and decide that external capital is the best option, the rest of this book is tailored for you. Chapter 3 explores the full range of funding options in more detail, so you can select the right type of capital for your specific situation.

If you conclude that you're not sure, that's useful information too. Read Chapter 3 anyway. The details on how each instrument actually works often clarify the decision more effectively than abstract questions can.

And if you decide that you don't need external capital, at least not yet, then the most valuable thing this chapter has done is save you from the opportunity cost of a fundraising process that would have consumed months of your time, energy, and focus. That is not a small thing.

3

Know Your Funding Options

Most founders approach funding as if there's only one product on the shelf. There isn't. There are several, and they work differently, cost different things, and they suit different situations. Picking the wrong one isn't a minor error. It can shape your company's future in ways that are very difficult to reverse.

This chapter outlines the full range of options available to founders seeking external capital. These options fall into three broad categories: equity instruments, where investors receive some ownership in your company; debt and revenue-based instruments, where capital is repaid over time without giving up equity; and non-dilutive options, where no equity changes hands and no debt is incurred. Understanding all three before you commit to any one of them is the whole point of this chapter.

Some options will be immediately relevant to you. Others won't suit your stage or your business model. The aim is to understand the full landscape before making any commitments, so that when you do choose, you choose deliberately.

Equity Instruments

Equity instruments give investors ownership in your company in exchange for capital. They are the most common form of startup funding and the most consequential, because the ownership you give up today affects every decision, every future funding round, and every exit scenario for the life of the company.

Angels and angel networks are where most founders start. An angel investor is an individual who invests their own money into early-stage companies. Cheque sizes vary widely. An individual angel might write a cheque for $10,000 or $500,000, depending on their appetite, their relationship with the founder, and the stage of the company. Angel networks, where groups of angels pool their evaluation and sometimes their capital, can collectively deploy larger amounts into a single round.

What angels offer beyond capital varies just as much. Some are former founders with genuine operational experience. Some have deep networks in your sector. Some write the cheque and then disappear. When you accept angel investment, you're often taking on the angel as much as the money. The quality of that relationship matters, particularly at the early stage when the business will face problems that money alone can't solve.

Angels typically invest through convertible notes or SAFEs, both explained in the next section. They rarely take formal board seats for smaller investments, although some negotiate an observer role or informal advisory access.

Pre-seed and seed funds are institutional investors who focus specifically on the earliest stages of company building. They are distinct from angel investors in that they manage pooled capital from limited partners, the institutional investors who back the fund itself, rather than investing their own money.

Pre-seed funds typically invest between $250,000 and $1 million. They support founders with a strong concept, early validation, and a credible team. They do not expect significant revenue; Instead, they bet on potential.

Seed funds typically invest between $1 million and $4 million, although check sizes can vary considerably. At this stage, they look for more evidence such as early customer traction, some revenue, or a product that clearly resonates with a defined group of users. Both pre-seed and seed funds will typically take a board seat or an observer seat, and will have protective provisions built into their investment terms.

Convertible notes and SAFEs are the instruments most commonly used in angel and seed rounds, so they belong here alongside the investors who use them rather than as a separate category.

A convertible note is a form of debt. The investor loans money to the company, and that debt converts into equity at a later stage, usually when the company raises a priced round. Two key terms determine how this conversion unfolds. The discount rate gives the note holder the right to convert at a lower price than the investors in the next round pay, typically 15 to 20 percent lower, as a reward for investing earlier and taking more risk. The valuation cap sets a maximum price at which the note converts, protecting the early investor if the company's valuation increases significantly before the next round.

When Airbnb raised its initial funding in 2009, it used convertible notes to attract small investments from angel investors before the first funding round was officially priced. The founders needed capital quickly, had no reliable way to value the company at that stage, and wanted to delay the valuation discussion until there was more evidence to base it on. Convertible notes let them do exactly that. The early angel investors who backed them converted into equity at a discount when the first priced round occurred, rewarding their early risk with a lower entry price than the new investors paid.

A SAFE, which stands for Simple Agreement for Future Equity, was developed by Y Combinator in 2013 and has become the dominant seed-stage instrument in many markets. A SAFE is not debt. It has no interest rate and no maturity date. The investor gives the company money now in exchange for the right to receive equity at a future priced round, on terms defined by a discount rate and a valuation cap. Stripe used SAFEs in its earliest funding rounds before its first institutional raise, a structure that let the founders move quickly, keep documentation simple, and focus on building rather than negotiating complex legal terms.

Because there is no interest accruing and no repayment date, SAFEs are simpler to administer than convertible notes. They are also faster to close and cheaper to document. For many seed rounds, particularly those involving multiple small angels, SAFEs have become the default instrument.

The risk for founders is the same with both instruments: the impact on the ownership structure is not fully clear until the conversion event occurs. Founders who combine multiple SAFEs with varying caps and discounts can find themselves in a more diluted position than they expected when a priced round finally happens. The example on the next page demonstrates how conversion works at different valuations and explains why the cap is more important than it first appears.

Series A institutional funds are a different category entirely. These are institutional rounds typically ranging from $5 million to $20 million, led by venture capital firms that are making a clear bet on a business that has already proven its model and is ready to scale.

Series A investors are not buying potential. They are buying evidence. They want to see consistent revenue growth, a repeatable process for acquiring customers, unit economics, meaning the revenue and cost generated by a single customer, that make sense at scale, and a management team with dedicated leaders across key functions, sales, product, engineering, and operations, rather than founders still covering multiple roles.

The due diligence process is more rigorous, the legal terms are more complex, and the governance expectations are more formal than at seed stage. The gap between seed and Series A is higher than most founders expect when they first encounter it. A founder who raises seed capital based on a strong team and $200,000 in annual recurring revenue will need to present a significantly different story to a Series A investor, who typically looks for $1 million to $3 million in annual recurring revenue growing at a strong and consistent rate.

How a Convertible Note or SAFE Converts

A worked numerical example showing two scenarios for a $250,000 SAFE with a $4 million cap and a 20% discount, converting at a $10 million Series A.

Scenario A: Without a cap

- Series A price per share: $1.00
- SAFE holder discount (20%): converts at $0.80 per share
- Shares received: 312,500
- Ownership at $10M valuation: 3.1%

Scenario B: With $4M cap (cap kicks in)

- Cap-implied price per share: $0.40 (based on $4M valuation)
- Shares received: 625,000
- Ownership at $10M valuation: 6.25%

The cap doubled the investor's equity stake. A liquidity event, meaning any transaction that returns capital to investors such as a sale or IPO, triggers the conversion calculation above. Founders with multiple SAFEs at different caps should model the full conversion impact, meaning the total ownership given up across all shares including options and convertible instruments, before accepting additional notes.

Debt and Revenue-Based Instruments

Not every form of external capital requires giving up ownership. Debt and revenue-based instruments provide capital that is repaid over time, leaving the founder's equity intact.

Revenue-based financing, sometimes called RBF, has grown significantly over the past decade and remains one of the most underused options by founders who would genuinely benefit from it. The mechanism is straightforward. A lender provides capital, typically between $100,000 and $5 million, in exchange for a fixed percentage of monthly revenue until a predetermined multiple of the original amount is repaid. A $500,000 investment at a 1.5x repayment cap would be fully repaid once $750,000 has been returned through the revenue share.

No equity changes hands. The founder retains full ownership. The cost is the revenue share, which reduces monthly cash flow until the obligation is cleared. This makes revenue-based financing most suitable for businesses with predictable, growing revenue and healthy margins. SaaS companies, subscription businesses, and e-commerce operations with high repeat-purchase rates are natural fits. Clearco and Lighter Capital are among the best-known providers globally. In Australia, providers including Choco Up and various fintech lenders have expanded access to this model. The application process is typically faster and less invasive than a venture raise, and there is no pitch, no partner meeting, and no term sheet negotiation. The lender looks at your revenue data and makes a decision.

Non-Dilutive Options

Non-dilutive capital is the category most founders walk past without looking. No equity. No debt. Capital in exchange for meeting specific conditions or providing specific value to a partner. For the right business, these options are among the best available.

Government grants are the most overlooked option on this list, and that oversight costs founders real money. Most dismiss them before they've looked properly, assuming the process is too slow or the criteria too narrow. That assumption is often wrong.

Non-dilutive capital, meaning capital that requires no equity and creates no debt, is available to founders in sectors including deep tech, biotech, clean energy, and advanced manufacturing. In Australia, the R&D Tax Incentive has returned significant cash to qualifying technology companies for development work they were doing regardless. The Accelerating Commercialisation program has provided up to $1 million to startups with novel, export-ready products. Canva received early-stage support through Western Australian government programs before it became the global platform it is today. The US Small Business Innovation Research program and the UK's Innovate UK fund technology and innovation projects across a wide range of sectors. The trade-off is time. Applications are thorough, reporting obligations are real, and the capital rarely arrives quickly. But if your business involves genuine research, novel technology, or software development, there is a real chance you qualify for something. The application costs time. The capital costs nothing.

Equity crowdfunding is worth considering for the right business, but it is not the right tool for most. Platforms such as Birchal and OnMarket in Australia, Seedrs and Crowdcube in the UK, and Wefunder and Republic in the US allow founders to raise funds from a large number of individual investors, often members of the public, in exchange for small equity stakes.

Here is the honest assessment. Equity crowdfunding works well for consumer-facing businesses with an existing community or a strong brand. A company whose customers are also passionate advocates can turn that community into a shareholder base, which creates both capital and a group of highly engaged supporters. For a B2B software company with no consumer profile, it is almost certainly the wrong fit. Managing a large number of small shareholders creates real administrative overhead. The fundraising process requires public disclosure of financial information that many founders prefer to keep private. And the round must be actively marketed, which takes time and money that early-stage founders rarely have in abundance. Know who your audience is before you consider this path.

Strategic partnerships are more accessible than most founders realise, and they are genuinely underused. A corporate partner, a supplier, a large potential customer, or an industry player who sees commercial value in your success may be willing to fund development in exchange for preferred access, co-development rights, or exclusivity in a specific market. This is not charity. It is a commercial arrangement where both parties see value that a purely financial investor cannot provide.

The challenge is that strategic partnerships require relationships that take time to build, and the terms need careful management to ensure you don't give away strategic control in exchange for capital. But when the right partner exists, the terms are often more favourable than any financial investor would offer, the network value is immediate, and the equity cost is zero.

Choosing Your Path

The right type of capital is not determined by what other founders in your space are doing. It's determined by three things specific to you: where your business is today, what you're trying to build, and what you're willing to trade to get there.

Work through these questions before you commit to any path.

What stage is your business at? If you have no revenue yet, revenue-based financing and most grant programs are not available to you. Your options are angels, pre-seed funding, strategic partnerships, or customer prepayments to generate early, committed revenue. If you have $500,000 or more in annual recurring revenue and it is growing, revenue-based financing becomes genuinely competitive with equity. If you are at $1 million to $3 million in revenue and growing fast, Series A is within reach.

What are you willing to trade? Equity permanently gives up ownership. Debt and revenue-based financing temporarily sacrifice cash flow. Grants require time. Strategic partnerships sometimes mean relinquishing exclusivity or preferred terms. Each trade carries different long-term costs. Assess the real impact on your ownership and cash flow before choosing the best option for your situation.

What does your business model require? A company that needs to move fast in a winner-takes-most market, where being second means being irrelevant, may genuinely need venture capital to succeed. A company with strong recurring revenue and modest capital requirements may find that revenue-based financing covers its growth needs entirely. A deep technology firm with a long development timeline may find that grants cover a significant portion of early costs before any equity raise is necessary.

There is no single right answer. There is only the answer that fits your specific situation honestly assessed. The chapters that follow go deeper into the process of raising equity capital, because for founders who have decided that equity is the right path, the process is specific and the preparation matters enormously. But the non-equity options in this chapter are not lesser alternatives. For some founders, in some situations, they are the better choice.

4

Getting Investor-Ready

There is a version of fundraising that most founders imagine before they go through it. You have a solid business, prepare a deck, secure some meetings, and the right investor sees what you see. A term sheet follows.

The reality is more demanding than that. Investors see hundreds of pitches. They are pattern-matching against every company they've seen before, every sector thesis they've formed, and every deal they've passed on that they wish they hadn't. In that environment, a founder who is not thoroughly prepared loses deals they should win, not because their business isn't good enough, but because they haven't packaged and presented the evidence in a way that makes an investor feel confident.

Getting investor-ready is the work you do before the first meeting. It is unglamorous, detail-heavy, and absolutely necessary. This chapter covers what that work looks like.

What Investors Actually Evaluate

Before you build anything, you need to understand what you're building it for. Investors at different stages are evaluating different things, and preparing the wrong evidence for the wrong audience is one of the most common reasons founders fail to close funding rounds.

At the seed stage, investors focus on five key questions. Who are these founders, and why are they the right people to tackle this problem? Is the problem real and large enough to build a meaningful business around? Is there proof that customers want what this company is developing? Can the founders clearly and credibly explain their target market? And does the company have a believable path to scale?

At Series A, the questions change. Revenue is now a given, and the investor wants to understand its quality and direction. Is revenue growing steadily, and can you explain why? Do you know what it costs to acquire a customer, and is that cost justified by the value that customer will bring over time? Is the process of attracting new customers repeatable, or does it rely on the founders personally closing every deal? And does the team have the operational depth, meaning dedicated leaders across sales, product, engineering, and operations rather than founders still covering multiple roles, to manage a company much larger than it is today?

These are different conversations. The preparation for each is different. Know which conversation you're about to have.

Building the Pitch

A pitch is not a product demo and it is not a business plan. It's a story. The best pitches tell a narrative with a clear beginning, middle, and end: highlighting a significant problem, explaining why we are the right people to solve it, showing evidence that we're on the right track, and outlining what we will do with your funding.

A typical pitch deck for a seed round comprises between ten and fifteen slides. For a Series A, it might be longer with more supporting data. The content should cover the following areas.

The problem. State it clearly and specifically. The most common mistake here is describing the problem in terms of the solution you've built rather than the pain the customer actually experiences. Investors want to feel the problem before they hear about your answer to it. When Airbnb created its original 2008 pitch deck, the problem slide did not lead with technology or a product concept. It described the specific frustration of travellers who couldn't find affordable, personal accommodation and hosts with spare space but no way to reach guests. The problem was human and immediate before the solution was mentioned. You can find that original deck by searching "Airbnb original 2008 pitch deck" on SlideShare, where it has been publicly available for years. Reading it alongside this chapter is worth twenty minutes of your time.

The solution. Explain what you've built and why it solves the problem better than the alternatives. This does not need to be a product walkthrough. It needs to be a clear articulation of the value you create. Airbnb's solution slide in that same deck was three words and a single image. Everything unnecessary had been removed.

The market. Investors need to believe there is a large enough opportunity to justify the risk. Total addressable market figures are fine, but the numbers that matter more are those that show your specific, reachable market and the share you can credibly capture. A company targeting a $50 billion market sounds impressive. A company that can clearly explain how to reach the first $10 million in revenue is more convincing.

The traction. This is your evidence slide. Revenue figures, growth rates, customer counts, retention data, net promoter scores, which measure how likely customers are to recommend your product to others on a scale of zero to ten, pilot agreements, and letters of intent. Whatever you have that shows the market is responding. Be specific and be honest. Investors have seen enough decks to spot inflated numbers and vague claims.

The business model. How do you generate revenue, and how does that scale? This doesn't need to be complicated, but it must be clear. Investors who can't understand how the business makes money won't feel confident enough to invest.

The team. Why you? This slide should explain why this specific group of people is exceptionally well-suited to succeed in this market. Domain expertise, relevant operating experience, complementary skills, and a proven track record all count here.

The ask. How much are you raising, what will you spend it on, and what milestone will that capital help you reach? The milestone is crucial. Investors want to know that the capital gets the business to a point where the next step, whether that's the next raise or profitability, becomes much easier.

The Narrative Test

Before you walk into any investor meeting, run your pitch through a simple test. Tell your story to someone who knows nothing about your business and ask them three questions afterwards.

What problem does this company solve? Who is the customer? Why will this company win?

If they can answer all three clearly and in their own words, your narrative is working. If they can't, you have more work to do. Investors hear dozens of pitches every month. The ones they remember and return to are the ones where the story was clear from the first telling. Run this test more than once, with different people, and treat any confusion in their answers as information about where your story breaks down rather than evidence that they weren't paying attention.

The Financial Story

There is a reason the financial story is separate from the pitch. The pitch is what gets you into the room. The financial story is what keeps you credible once you're there. A founder who tells a compelling story and then stumbles on basic financial questions loses the confidence they built in the first ten minutes. Know these six numbers before you walk into any investor conversation.

Revenue is the starting point for every investor conversation. Know your current monthly and annual recurring revenue, your growth rate over the past six to twelve months, and your revenue mix if you have multiple products or customer segments.

Burn rate answers a simple question: how much cash do you spend each month beyond what you earn? Know this number precisely. Investors will ask, and a founder who hesitates on their own burn rate signals to the room that they are not on top of the business.

Runway tells you and your investors how long the business can operate at its current burn rate before it runs out of money. Twelve months or more is the minimum you want to raise when you start raising. Six months is a crisis, and investors can smell it.

Customer Acquisition Cost, or CAC, is what it costs you on average to bring in one new customer. Include all sales and marketing expenses in this calculation, not just the obvious line items. A founder who quotes only their paid advertising spend and forgets their sales team's salaries is understating their true CAC and will be caught out on it.

Customer Lifetime Value, or LTV, is the total revenue you expect to generate from a customer over the full period they remain a customer. The LTV-to-CAC ratio is one of the most important indicators of business health. A ratio of 3:1 or better, meaning each customer generates at least three times what they cost to acquire, is generally considered healthy at the growth stage.

Gross margin is the percentage of revenue remaining after deducting the direct costs of delivering your product or service. Software businesses typically operate at 70 to 80 percent gross margin, while service businesses tend to have lower margins. Investors use this metric to evaluate how the business will perform at scale, because a business with a strong gross margin has a fundamentally different path to profitability compared to one with thin margins.

If you are pre-revenue, you won't have exact numbers for CAC, LTV, or gross margin yet. That's fine at the seed stage. The key is that you understand what these metrics are, why they matter, and how you'll measure them once you have customers. Investors backing early-stage companies know the data is limited. They want to see if you understand your own business model well enough to track the important metrics as it grows.

The graphic on the next page shows how these metrics connect and what the healthy ranges look like at each stage.

The Key Numbers Every Investor Will Ask About

A connected framework showing the metrics, their definitions, and healthy benchmarks by stage:

Metric	What it measures	Seed benchmark	Series A benchmark
Monthly Revenue	What the business earns	Some evidence of paying customers	$80K-$250K MRR and growing
Burn Rate	Monthly cash spent beyond revenue	Lean, justified by stage	Clearly tied to growth investment
Runway	Months of capital remaining	12+ months post-raise	18+ months post-raise
CAC	Cost to acquire one customer	Rough estimate based on early data	Clearly calculated and declining
LTV	Revenue from one customer over time	Estimated from early patterns	Demonstrated from cohort data, meaning tracked groups of customers acquired in the same period, showing how their spending evolves over time
LTV:CAC Ratio	Efficiency of growth spend	2:1 or better	3:1 or better
Gross Margin	Revenue minus direct delivery costs	Positive direction clear	50%+ (70%+ for SaaS)

Early-stage benchmarks are directional. Strong founders who can explain the trajectory matter more than hitting every number precisely.

The Data Room

After a successful first meeting, serious investors will want to go deeper. The data room is where you give them access to the documents that let them do that. Having it ready before you need it is the difference between a smooth process and one that stalls while you scramble to find two-year-old contracts.

What a data room communicates goes beyond its contents. A founder who responds to a due diligence request within 24 hours with a clean, clearly organised folder of complete documents tells the investor something important: this person runs a tidy operation and knows where everything is. A founder who takes five days to assemble a partial set of documents with inconsistent naming and missing pages tells a different story. Investors who encounter the second type frequently revisit their enthusiasm, even when the business itself is strong.

A data room for a seed round usualy includes: incorporation documents and a current cap table showing all shares, including options and any convertible instruments, financial statements for the past two years if available, monthly management accounts for the current year, customer contracts or anonymised customer data, product screenshots or a demo environment, and any intellectual property registrations or pending applications.

A Series A data room is more comprehensive. At this stage, you'll have more history to share, and investors will expect it. This typically includes everything mentioned earlier, plus audited accounts, a detailed financial model with assumptions, a full customer list with revenue per customer, employment agreements for key staff, and existing investor agreements. If you're currently raising seed funding, none of this is required yet. Save it for later and prepare for it.

Tools like Notion, Google Drive, or dedicated data room platforms like Docsend or Caplinked all work. The format matters less than the organisation. A data room that is hard to navigate signals disorganisation in the business. One that is clean, clearly labelled, and complete signals a founder who is on top of their company.

A Real Example of Getting It Right

When Canva, the Australian design platform, raised its first significant institutional round in 2013, the founders had been meticulous about preparation. Melanie Perkins had spent two years building relationships with investors, refining the pitch, and accumulating specific evidence of user demand before the capital followed.

The investors who passed early, and many did, gave feedback that was incorporated into subsequent conversations. By the time a term sheet arrived, the pitch had been tested, sharpened, and supported by evidence that made the opportunity clear. Canva went on to raise over $500 million in subsequent rounds and reach a valuation of $40 billion. The groundwork laid in those early preparation stages shaped how the company was received at every subsequent raise.

Getting investor-ready is not about performing competence. It is about building it, then communicating it clearly. Those are two different tasks, and both require deliberate work.

5

Finding the Right Investors

Most fundraising advice focuses on how to pitch. This chapter emphasises something more important: who you pitch to, and in what order.

Getting in front of the wrong investor is not neutral. It wastes time that early-stage founders cannot afford to waste, it consumes the energy and focus that the business needs, and it can create a trail of passes that shapes how later investors perceive you. The startup investing world is connected enough that a pattern of rejections from well-known funds becomes information that travels.

Choosing whom to approach, in what sequence, and through which channel is a strategic decision. This chapter provides you with the framework to do it well.

Why Fit Matters More Than Fame

The first instinct many founders have is to target the most well-known investors in their market. The biggest fund name, the most prominent partner, the investor whose portfolio reads like a list of companies they admire. This is understandable and almost always the wrong starting point.

Investor fit isn't about prestige. It's about alignment on three specific things: stage, sector, and style.

Stage means the investor backs companies at the same stage of development as yours. A fund that leads Series B rounds is not the right target for a founder raising seed capital, no matter how well the pitch lands. Some investors are flexible across stages. Most are not. Approaching an investor at the wrong stage signals that you haven't done basic research, which is not the impression you want to create.

Sector means the investor has a genuine interest and ideally some knowledge of the space you're building in. An investor who has backed three healthcare companies and speaks publicly about the opportunity in digital health is more likely to understand your pitch, move faster, and add value after the investment than a generalist who finds your space interesting but has never operated in it.

Style is the hardest to assess from the outside and the most important to get right. Some investors are genuinely collaborative partners who add value between meetings and pick up the phone when things are hard. Others are largely passive until something goes wrong, at which point they become very active in ways you may not welcome. The difference is not always visible from a fund's website or their public profile.

How to Research Investors Properly

Start with the public record before you contact anyone. Crunchbase and PitchBook show you what a fund has actually backed, at what stage, and how recently. LinkedIn shows you the partner who led each deal and who they know in common with you. In Australia, Cut Through Venture tracks local VC activity with enough granularity to tell you which funds are actively deploying right now versus those that have slowed their pace. In the US, CB Insights and the NVCA track investment trends at a sector and stage level. None of this replaces a direct conversation. But walking into that conversation knowing the fund's last five investments, the partner's background, and the stage they prefer is a different experience from walking in cold.

Look at their portfolio companies, not just the logos on the website, but the actual businesses. What stage were those companies in when the investor first backed them? What have those companies achieved since? Are any operating in markets related to yours? A portfolio company founder who's experienced the investor's approach firsthand is your most valuable research resource.

Look at the investor's activity over the past twelve months. Investors who have been actively writing cheques recently are more likely to be deploying capital now. Investors who made most of their investments three years ago and have few recent deals may be in harvest mode, meaning they are focused on managing existing investments and returning capital to their own investors, the institutions and individuals who back the fund itself, rather than making new bets.

Also read the thesis carefully. If an investor has publicly stated that they focus on B2B software with strong network effects and you're developing a consumer marketplace, move on. They are making it clear what they support. Founders who ignore the published thesis waste their own time and the investor's.

Finding Portfolio Founders Who Will Tell You the Truth

Here is the most important research step most founders skip. Before you approach any investor, talk to the founders in their portfolio. Not the ones the investor suggests. The ones you find yourself.

The founders an investor introduces you to have been pre-selected. They are almost always the ones with the best relationship with that investor, the ones most likely to say positive things. That is not useful information.

Go to the investor's portfolio page and identify companies at a similar stage to yours. Find the founders of those companies on LinkedIn. Send a brief, straightforward message explaining that you are considering taking investment from their investor and would appreciate fifteen minutes of honest advice. Most founders will reply. The startup community strongly encourages paying help forward.

Ask three questions. What did the investor do when times were tough? How often did they add value beyond just the capital? And is there anything you wish you had known before accepting their money?

Those answers will tell you more about the investor than any pitch meeting ever will.

Two Founders Who Got This Right

Understanding investor fit in the abstract is useful. Seeing how two founders applied it in practice is even more useful.

Reid Hoffman approached LinkedIn's early fundraising with a level of deliberateness that was unusual at the time. Rather than pitching broadly and hoping for the best, he was unusually selective about which investors he spoke to. He focused on firms that understood network-effect businesses, looked for partners with operating experience who could serve as useful board members rather than just capital providers, and targeted funds whose stage appetite matched where LinkedIn actually was.

He didn't treat fundraising as a one-off sales pitch. He spent time building relationships with investors he respected, came into discussions with specific questions about how they worked and where they could help, and evaluated potential investors as seriously as he expected them to evaluate him. Greylock Partners went on to lead LinkedIn's Series B round in 2004, and Hoffman later joined the firm as a partner. He has written and spoken about this philosophy of choosing investors and financing growth extensively in his book *Blitzscaling* and across multiple episodes of his *Masters of Scale* podcast, both of which are worth reading alongside this chapter.

Melanie Perkins took a different path to achieve a similar result. When she was raising funds for Canva in the early 2010s, she had no existing investor network in the United States and was based in Perth, a city far from the usual tech-investment hubs. Instead of seeing that as a permanent barrier, she approached it as a problem to solve systematically.

She spent years traveling, attending events, and building relationships with global investors, including trips to places where Silicon Valley backers naturally gathered. Along the way, she met venture capitalist Bill Tai, who became one of Canva's early supporters and helped connect her with technical talent and other backers. She spent about two years making introductions, asking for perspective rather than capital, and demonstrating traction with early users. By the time she was ready for a formal institutional round, she had built a warm network of investors who already understood what Canva could do.

The eventual Series A round, led by Matrix Partners in 2015, did not happen because of a last-minute cold pitch; it happened because the relationships were already in place. The pitch came after the trust.

What both stories share is purposefulness. Neither founder pitched randomly and hoped the right investor would emerge. Both mapped the landscape, identified the right targets, built the necessary relationships to reach them, and treated the process as a strategic campaign rather than a series of isolated events.

Building the Target List

Once you've researched your options, create a tiered list. Not every investor is equally worth approaching, and the order in which you approach them is important.

Tier one is your primary targets: investors who are the right stage and sector fit, whose portfolio founders spoke well of them, and who have been actively deploying capital recently. These are the investors you want to anchor the round. A commitment from a tier one investor creates momentum that makes every subsequent conversation easier, partly because investors pay attention to what other investors are interested in. In a venture portfolio, a small number of investments generate the majority of returns, which means funds pay close attention to what their peers are backing. A tier one lead signals quality to everyone who follows.

Tier two is strong secondary targets: investors who are a good fit, but where there is some uncertainty. Perhaps their last investment in your sector was two years ago, or their typical check size is slightly smaller than you need. These are worth pursuing in parallel once you have some momentum.

Tier three is exploratory: investors who are a plausible fit, but where you have less conviction. These conversations are useful for feedback and for sharpening your pitch, but don't build your raise around them.

A realistic seed round target list might include eight to twelve tier one investors, ten to fifteen tier two, and a few from tier three. These numbers reflect the typical conversion rate from first meeting to term sheet, which is about one in ten to one in fifteen for most founders at seed stage. Working backwards from the goal of securing one or two term sheets to close a round, you need enough discussions underway to reach that target without relying on any single investor saying yes. A Series A list is usually more targeted, as the number of funds active at that stage in any market tends to be smaller.

Timing and Sequencing

The way you approach investors influences how the raise unfolds. There are several principles worth understanding.

Don't approach your top targets first. The early conversations in a raise are where you'll receive the most useful feedback and where your pitch will improve the quickest. Investor questions reveal gaps in your story that you hadn't anticipated. Objections you hear in the first week will be ones you can prepare for in the third week. Running those early conversations with tier two or tier three targets means you arrive at your best opportunities with a tighter story, sharper answers to the hard questions, and more confidence in how the narrative lands. A pitch in its third iteration is significantly better than the same pitch in its first.

Create natural momentum by running multiple conversations in parallel rather than one after the other. An investor who knows other investors are looking at the same company is more likely to move at a reasonable pace. An investor who knows they are your only current conversation has little reason to hurry. This is not manipulation. It is the natural dynamic of any market where demand indicates value.

Be honest about where you are in the process without manufacturing false urgency. If another investor has shown strong interest, it's fair to mention that. If no one has moved yet, don't pretend otherwise. Investors talk to each other, and credibility is worth more than artificial pressure.

The Warm Introduction

The startup investment scene runs on warm introductions. A referral from someone the investor already knows and trusts, which is what a warm introduction is, does three things simultaneously. It increases the chances of your email being opened rather than filtered. It offers an implicit endorsement before you say a word. And it creates a social obligation for the investor to agree to the meeting.

The best sources of warm introductions, roughly in order of effectiveness, are other founders the investor has backed, lawyers who regularly work in the venture space, accountants and advisors with relationships with investors, accelerator program managers, and other investors who are not competing for the same deal.

Building the network required to get these introductions takes time. The founders who raise funds most effectively are the ones who began cultivating investor relationships twelve to eighteen months before they needed capital. They attended the right events, connected with the right people, and were helpful to others before they needed anything in return. Both Reid Hoffman and Melanie Perkins did this. Neither of them started the process when they needed the money.

What to Do When You Don't Have the Network

Some founders approach fundraising without the connections that make warm introductions easy. This is more typical outside major startup hubs and represents a real structural barrier rather than a personal failing.

Accelerators are specifically designed to close this gap. Programs like Y Combinator, Startmate in Australia, and Entrepreneur First in the UK exist partly to solve the warm introduction problem for founders who don't yet have the network. The cost is equity, typically between one and seven percent of the company, which is a meaningful amount to give up for access alone. Whether that trade is worth making depends on the specific program, the stage you're at, and the strength of your existing investor relationships. For a founder with no network and a genuinely early business, the right accelerator can compress years of relationship-building into three months. For a founder who already has strong investor connections, the equity cost may not be justified.

Beyond accelerators, identify the lawyers, accountants, and advisors in your market who work regularly with startups and investors. Building a relationship with one of these professionals, who may already have relationships with the investors you want to meet, is often more efficient than trying to reach investors directly.

Write publicly about what you're building and the problems you're solving. Investors read more than most people realise, and a well-argued post about a market insight or a product decision creates visibility with an audience you could not reach through direct outreach alone.

And don't underestimate other founders. A warm introduction from a well-regarded founder who has worked alongside you or knows your work can carry as much weight as an introduction from an advisor or lawyer.

The First Conversation

The first conversation with an investor isn't a pitch. It's a meeting. There is a difference.

Go in with the aim of creating a genuine dialogue rather than delivering a presentation. Understand what the investor is working on and what they find interesting. Ask questions as well as answering them. The founders who leave the strongest impression in first meetings are usually the ones who demonstrate clarity of thought, listen carefully, and assess the relationship as critically as the investor does.

Come prepared to answer the hard questions: what is your biggest risk, what are you most uncertain about, and what would have to be true for this not to work? Investors who ask these questions are doing their job well. Founders who answer them honestly and thoughtfully earn significantly more trust than founders who deflect or pivot to safer ground.

By the end of the first meeting, know what the next step is. If the investor is interested, there should be a clear path forward: a follow-up call, a meeting with a partner, or a request for specific data. If there is no next step, ask for one directly. "What would need to be true for you to want to meet again?" is a straightforward question that cuts through the politeness that can often obscure a soft pass. Ambiguity after a first meeting usually works in the investor's favour, not yours.

6

The Pitch and the Process

Fundraising is a process, not just a single event. Most founders see it as a series of separate pitch meetings, each one a new effort to impress a different audience. Successful founders approach it as a managed campaign, which means a planned sequence of conversations happening at the same time with multiple investors, featuring a clear start, a deliberate middle, and a controlled close.

The difference in outcomes between the two approaches is significant. Founders who understand the full process — what happens at each stage, what investors are trying to learn, and how to build momentum across multiple conversations — raise funds faster, on better terms, and with less damage to their business. Those who don't often spend six months in a demoralising cycle of meetings that lead nowhere, while their runway shortens and their team questions what's going on.

This chapter walks you through the process from first contact to signed term sheet and gives you the tools to manage it effectively.

What the Investor Is Doing on Their Side

Before covering what you should do, it helps to understand what is happening on the investor's side of the table. Not because it's interesting as an organisational matter, but because misreading the investor's process is one of the most reliable sources of founder anxiety during a raise. Founders who understand what is happening internally stop interpreting silence as rejection and stop chasing investors who have already decided to pass.

Most founders see fundraising as a series of conversations with just one person. What they don't notice is the internal process that decides whether that chat leads anywhere.

Most institutional funds involve multiple people in a single investment decision. An associate or analyst may screen initial opportunities. A junior partner may take the first meeting and draft an internal memo. The entire partnership reviews opportunities at a weekly or fortnightly meeting. A partner must champion the deal internally with enough confidence to bring it to the group. Due diligence includes legal, financial, and sometimes technical reviews. The final investment decision often requires the agreement of all or most partners.

This process takes time. It can be six to twelve weeks from the first meeting to a term sheet at the seed stage, and three to six months at Series A. The practical takeaway for founders is straightforward: a second meeting doesn't equate to strong interest. It simply means the investor hasn't decided to pass yet. A request for more data isn't a sign of intent to buy; it's just a data request. An investor who says "we'd love to stay close" has almost certainly decided to pass. The only signal that counts is a term sheet.

If you need capital in eight weeks, you should have started this process four months ago.

The Typical Process Stage by Stage

While each investor and each raise may vary slightly, the sequence below outlines what most institutional raises typically look like from initial contact to closing.

First contact and initial meeting. This usually lasts 30 to 45 minutes, often over video call, and aims to provide the investor with enough information to decide whether to explore further. They are evaluating the team first, the market second, and the traction third. Your goal is to tell a clear story, demonstrate a thorough understanding of your market, and agree on a clear next step.

Follow-up and second meeting. If the investor is interested, they will ask for more. A follow-up call to go deeper on specific questions, a meeting with additional partners, access to your data room, or customer references. Each is a step in the investor's internal evaluation process. Respond promptly and completely. Investors who are genuinely interested move relatively quickly. Investors who ask for more and then go quiet are usually working their way toward a pass.

Partner meeting. At most institutional funds, a meeting with the full partnership is a positive signal. It means the deal has been championed internally and the fund is doing its final evaluation. Treat this meeting as seriously as the first. The questions will be sharper and the room will be more sceptical, because the partners who haven't met you yet have not yet been won over.

Due diligence. If the partner meeting goes well, the fund will move into due diligence, which involves a thorough review of the claims made in the pitch, including financial statements, customer references, legal structure, intellectual property, and team backgrounds. Be prepared for this process to feel invasive; it often is. The best response is to be fully transparent and respond quickly. Investors who find founders who are slow, evasive, or disorganised during due diligence often pass on the opportunity, even if they were enthusiastic before it started.

Term sheet. A signed term sheet marks the point where the process shifts from evaluation to negotiation. It is not a binding commitment to invest, but it is a serious expression of intent, and in most markets, it comes with an exclusivity period during which you agree not to negotiate with other investors. Chapter 7 covers what to look for in a term sheet in detail.

Brian Chesky has spoken extensively about Airbnb's early fundraising experience, both in interviews and in Leigh Gallagher's book *The Airbnb Story*. When Airbnb was raising its initial seed and early-round capital around 2009–2010, the company was rejected by many of the investors they approached. The feedback from those early conversations was not encouraging.

In 2009, Airbnb closed a seed round of about $600,000, with Sequoia Capital and a small group of others backing the idea despite scepticism in the broader market. That round gave them runway to keep iterating and refining the product while they worked to turn early interest into repeaters.

Chesky and his co-founders kept listening to what they were hearing. The story became clearer. The evidence became more compelling. Their metrics, documents, and supporting data became more organised. The conversations they had later in the process were received differently than the ones at the start, not because the business had fundamentally changed in those months, but because the founders' ability to articulate what the business was had improved dramatically through the experience of being challenged by people who said no.

In 2010, Airbnb raised a Series A round of about 7.2 million dollars, again led by Sequoia Capital. That round marked a turning point: investors who had previously declined now saw a clearer pattern of growth and a more coherent story. The lesson Chesky has repeatedly emphasised is that the process itself—including the rejections—was what made the pitch successful. Readers who want the full account can search for "Brian Chesky Airbnb fundraising" alongside *The Airbnb Story*.

Questions Founders Should Ask

Most founders treat investor meetings as one-directional. The investor asks questions, the founder answers them. This is a mistake for two reasons.

First, asking good questions shows strategic thinking. A founder who asks an investor about their decision-making process, their involvement in difficult situations, and their portfolio construction approach communicates that they assess relationships rather than just accepting capital from anyone who offers it. That impression matters.

Second, you genuinely need the answers. You're considering entering a relationship that could last seven to ten years and that gives the other party real influence over your business. Gathering the information necessary to make that decision properly is not optional.

Here are the important questions worth asking in early investor conversations.

What does your involvement look like after the investment closes? Some investors are highly engaged. Others are largely passive until something goes wrong. Neither is inherently wrong, but you need to know which you're getting.

Can you tell me about a company in your portfolio that went through a difficult period? What did you do? This question reveals more about an investor's character than any other question you can ask. Listen for whether they talk about their own actions or the company's actions. Listen for whether they stayed constructive under pressure.

What would need to be true for you to lead this round? This cuts directly to the evaluation criteria and tells you what the investor needs to see to move forward. It also tells you whether a lead is possible at all.

How many new investments did your fund make last year, and how many are you planning this year? This tells you whether the fund is actively deploying capital or approaching the end of its investment period.

What is your fund's usual timeline for requiring a return on an investment like this? This highlights the timing question that influences almost every key decision in the investor relationship: a founder wanting to build for fifteen years and a fund needing a return within seven are not inherently aligned. It's better to know this before you sign.

Managing Multiple Conversations

Running a single-track fundraising process, meaning approaching one investor at a time and waiting for their answer before moving to the next, is one of the most common strategic mistakes founders make. It takes two to three times as long as running parallel conversations and it produces no competitive dynamic that gives any investor a reason to move.

The reason parallel conversations matter goes deeper than efficiency. In a VC portfolio, a small number of investments generate the majority of returns. Every fund is trying to find and secure those outliers before their peers do. When an investor knows that other credible investors are also evaluating the same company, the dynamic shifts. The timeline compresses because no serious investor wants to lose a deal they like to a competitor. The terms improve because a founder with options negotiates from a different position than a founder with none. Parallel conversations create that dynamic legitimately. Sequential ones produce no competitive signal and give every investor unlimited time to decide.

The aim is to run multiple conversations at the same time so your most serious prospects are roughly in the same stage of the process simultaneously. To create this Situation, you need to start your outreach across your entire target list within a short period, usually two to three weeks. Not all at once, but in a coordinated way that ensures your tier one and tier two conversations are underway before any of them have had time to fully evaluate and respond.

This does not mean manufacturing false urgency or misrepresenting your position. It means being organised and proactive. If an investor asks whether others are looking at the company, you can honestly say yes if they are. If an investor asks whether you have a term sheet, tell them the truth. Investors verify these things, and credibility lost in a raise is very hard to recover.

Building and Communicating Momentum

Momentum in a fundraise is real and it compounds. An investor who hears that two other credible investors are interested behaves differently than one who believes they are the only ones in the conversation.

Build momentum by being specific and honest in how you communicate your process. When a first meeting goes well, follow up within 24 hours with a clear summary of what you discussed and the next steps you agreed on. When an investor asks for something, deliver it faster than they expect. When another investor shows strong interest, it's appropriate to let your other active conversations know that the process is progressing.

What you should not do is invent momentum that doesn't exist. Telling an investor that you have a term sheet when you don't, or that another fund is close to committing when they are not, is a misrepresentation that can end a deal immediately if discovered. In a connected ecosystem, it usually is.

Common Process Mistakes

There are patterns that can derail otherwise strong fundraises. Most of them are avoidable.

Starting too late is the mistake that makes every other mistake worse. A founder with four months of runway cannot afford to let a promising conversation develop at its natural pace. They cannot walk away from bad terms. They cannot run a second process if the first one stalls. Twelve months of runway is the minimum at which a raise feels like a choice rather than a crisis. The founders who get the best outcomes almost always started earlier than felt necessary at the time.

Pitching the wrong investors first wastes your best opportunities when your pitch is least developed. Early investor conversations are where your story gets tested against real scepticism for the first time. Objections you hear in week one are ones you can prepare for in week three. Run those early conversations with tier two or tier three targets and arrive at your best opportunities with a pitch that has already been sharpened by the process.

Letting conversations go cold is a slow and unseen way of undermining yourself. A first meeting that goes well can fade away if neglected. Follow up promptly, maintain the momentum, and keep investors who show interest updated on your progress. An investor who loses sight of your progress might assume your momentum has stalled.

Overloading the first meeting with detail mistakes the purpose of that conversation. The goal of a first meeting is to earn a second one. Founders who try to cover everything in the first conversation lose the investor's attention before they reach the most compelling part. Tell the essential story clearly and leave room for questions.

Misreading a soft pass, meaning an indirect decline, costs weeks of wasted energy. Investors rarely say no directly. They say "the timing isn't right" or "we'd love to stay close" or "let's reconnect in a few months." These are passes. Treat them as such, thank the investor, keep the relationship warm, and move on. Continuing to pursue an investor who has softly declined consumes energy you need elsewhere.

Negotiating against yourself is the trap of discomfort with silence. Some founders, uncomfortable with no response after a strong meeting, start offering more favourable terms before the investor has asked for them. Wait. Let the investor make the first move on terms. If they are interested, they will.

Spreading your attention across too many low-quality conversations at once is the opposite of handling too few. A target list should be large enough to offer real options but focused enough to give each conversation the attention it deserves. Twenty simultaneous conversations, poorly managed, lead to worse results than twelve managed well.

A Real Example of Process Done Well

The Atlassian story is relevant here not because it was a typical raise, but because it illustrates what happens when founders begin the process from a position of genuine strength.

Mike Cannon-Brookes and Scott Farquhar spent years building a profitable business before taking any external capital. Atlassian was self-funded and generating strong revenue—about $58 million in the 2010 financial year—before its first institutional round.

In 2010, the company brought in a $60 million minority investment from Accel Partners. The business was already profitable, had over 20,000 customers, and employed hundreds of people across Australia, North America, and Europe. The founders used the capital partly for founder and employee liquidity, partly to accelerate expansion into Europe and Asia, and partly to pursue strategic acquisitions—all while retaining control.

The connection to this chapter's principles is clear. Atlassian did not start the fundraising process too late, nor did it pitch from a position of weakness. The founders did not manufacture urgency or accept the first term sheet out of nerves. They chose their investor carefully, negotiated from a position of strength, and kept the control and alignment that only come when founders aren't desperate for cash.

Atlassian went public on the Nasdaq in 2015, valued at about $5.8 billion at IPO. Both Cannon-Brookes and Farquhar retained significant equity stakes and continued to lead the company, showing that disciplined, founder-backed growth can still deliver a blockbuster outcome.

Run the process as if you have options, even before you do. Then build the options as fast as you can.

7

What You're Actually Signing

A term sheet arrives, and most first-time founders do one of two things. They either read it carefully but understand very little of it, or they hand it straight to their lawyer and wait for a summary. Both responses leave money and control on the table.

Your lawyer is essential. This chapter is not an argument for going without one. But founders who rely entirely on legal counsel in a term sheet negotiation are outsourcing their judgment. A lawyer can explain what a clause means. Only you can decide whether it aligns with what you're trying to build. And you can't make that judgment without understanding what you're reading.

This chapter gives you that understanding. It focuses on the terms that genuinely affect outcomes, explains them clearly, outlines what each term signals about the investor who is asking for it, and shows you where the traps are. The rest, which makes up most of a typical term sheet, is mostly noise.

The Foundation: Two Types of Shares

Before anything else, you need to understand the distinction that underpins every term in this chapter.

When investors put money into your company, they receive **preferred stock**. When founders start the company and employees are granted equity, they hold **common stock**. These are not equal. Preferred stock comes with special rights: priority in receiving proceeds when the company is sold, protection against dilution in certain scenarios, and in many cases veto rights over major decisions. Common stock sits below preferred stock in the order of priority. It is what founders and employees hold, and its value in any exit scenario depends entirely on what remains after the preferred stockholders have claimed their entitlements.

Almost every term in a standard term sheet describes the specific rights attached to the preferred stock the investor receives. Understanding that distinction makes the rest of the chapter significantly easier to follow.

The Two Categories That Matter

Term sheets can be twenty or thirty pages long and contain dozens of provisions. Most of them are not very significant in practice. Almost everything falls into one of two categories that truly impact founders, while the rest mainly cover edge cases that rarely happen.

Those two categories are **economics** and **control**.

Economic terms determine how the company's financial proceeds are divided when an event occurs: a sale, a liquidation, an IPO, or a down round. Control terms determine who makes key decisions about the company's direction. Get these right, and the rest is manageable. Get them wrong, and no amount of favourable language elsewhere in the document will fix it.

Valuation and the Option Pool Shuffle

Valuation is what most founders focus on first, and it matters. But it is probably the least important of the major terms, because several other provisions can render it economically meaningless in realistic exit scenarios.

Pre-money valuation is what the investor values the company at before the investment. Post-money valuation adds the investment on top. These numbers determine the investor's ownership percentage. An investor putting $2 million into a company at an $8 million pre-money valuation owns 20 percent of a $10 million post-money company.

The option pool shuffle is a common valuation trap and it belongs here alongside valuation because it directly affects what founders actually own after the deal closes. Investors often require that an unissued employee option pool, typically 10 to 20 percent of the fully diluted share count, meaning all shares, including options and any convertible instruments, be included in the pre-money valuation rather than the post-money valuation. This effectively means the pool is taken out of the founders' stake before the investment, not after. An $8 million pre-money valuation that requires a 15 percent option pool to be set aside first is effectively a lower valuation than it appears. Model the actual founder ownership percentage after all dilution before celebrating a headline number.

When an investor demands a large option pool in the pre-money, consider what they might be signalling. It often shows a genuine belief that the company needs to hire extensively. Sometimes, it indicates an attempt to lower their effective entry price at the founder's expense. Determining which situation applies involves asking directly why the pool is set at that size and which specific hires it aims to cover.

Liquidation Preferences

This is the term that has the most direct financial impact on what founders receive when the company is sold. It causes more unpleasant surprises than any other provision in a term sheet, and it is the one most worth understanding in precise numerical terms before you sign anything.

When Facebook acquired Instagram in 2012 for about 1 billion dollars, the way the proceeds were distributed was shaped significantly by the liquidation preferences held by Instagram's investors. Early reports and later analyses, including those in Sarah Frier's book No Filter, suggest that the preference structure meant the distribution of that billion dollars was not simply proportional to ownership percentages. Early investors with preference rights typically received their returns before common-stock holders, which included many employees who had joined the company expecting a more straightforward, share-like payout.

The exact dollar-by-dollar split among investor classes is not fully public, but the structural pattern is clear: two founders with the same ownership percentages in two different deals can receive dramatically different amounts from the same sale price, depending on the liquidation-preference architecture sitting above their common stock.

The key lesson isn't that Instagram's outcome was poor. In fact, it was a transformative, life-changing exit for many. The crucial point is that **ownership percentage alone is not the full picture**; the preference stack and deal structure can quietly reshape who actually benefits from a headline-round headline sale.

A liquidation preference determines how sale proceeds are distributed before common shareholders, meaning founders and employees, receive anything.

A **1x non-participating liquidation preference** is typical. It means the investor recovers their original investment before anyone else receives any payout. If the sale proceeds are substantial enough, the investor converts their preferred stock to common stock and shares proportionally with everyone else. In a strong exit, this clause is mostly unnoticed. An investor requesting a 1x non-participating is signalling that they expect the investment to perform well and are not primarily concerned with protecting against downside.

A **1x participating liquidation preference** is considerably more aggressive. The investor gets their original investment back first, and then also shares in the remaining proceeds alongside common shareholders. This is known as double-dipping, and it can dramatically reduce what founders and employees receive in all but the largest exits. An investor who asks for participation rights is signalling, whether intentionally or not, that they are more concerned with protecting their downside than on building toward a big outcome. It's important to be aware of this before signing.

A **2x participating liquidation preference** is even more aggressive. The investor gets twice their investment back before anyone else receives anything, and then participates in the remainder.

The graphic below shows these scenarios side by side to make the impact visible.

How Liquidation Preferences Change Founder Outcomes

Three scenarios using the same deal: $3M investment, 25% ownership, $15M exit.

	1x Non-Participating	1x Participating	2x Participating
Investor takes first	$3M	$3M	$6M
Remaining proceeds	$12M	$12M	$9M
Investor's proportional share	Converts to common: $3M	Additional 25%: $3M	Additional 25%: $2.25M
Total to investor	$6M	$6M	$8.25M
Total to founders and employees	$9M	$9M	$6.75M
Founder impact vs. standard	Baseline	Same at this exit size	$2.25M less

The difference becomes much more pronounced at smaller exit sizes. For example, with a $6 million exit and a 2x participating preference, the investor receives all the proceeds, and the founders get nothing.

Push back on any participation right above 1x non-participating. It is negotiable at the seed stage in most markets, and founders who accept aggressive participation terms without attempting to negotiate often leave significant value on the table.

Anti-Dilution Provisions

Anti-dilution provisions protect investors if the company raises a subsequent round at a lower valuation than the round they participated in. This is called a down round, and these provisions determine how the investor's ownership stake is adjusted when one happens.

During the dot-com bust of 2000 and 2001, dozens of companies that had raised capital at peak valuations found themselves needing to raise again at dramatically lower ones. Founders and employees at companies with full ratchet anti-dilution provisions in their early investor agreements experienced severe dilution in those down rounds, sometimes losing most of their remaining equity in a single financing event. The difference between full ratchet and broad-based weighted average was often the key factor in whether founders retained a meaningful stake or lost nearly everything. These cases are documented across multiple accounts from the dot-com era, and they are the reason why full ratchet provisions are now considered a major red flag in most markets.

Full ratchet anti-dilution is the most aggressive form available and the one most damaging to founders. It works like this: if a single share is sold in a down round at a lower price, the investor's entire position reprices to match. One share. The entire investment. The dilution to founders and employees can be catastrophic, and it is triggered by a threshold so low that almost any down round qualifies. If a full ratchet appears in a term sheet, treat it as a significant signal about what the investor expects the future to look like. An investor who insists on full ratchet protection is telling you they are genuinely worried about a down round scenario. That belief is worth taking seriously regardless of whether you share it.

Broad-based weighted average anti-dilution is the market standard and is much less harsh. It adjusts the conversion price using a formula that accounts for the size of the down round, rather than revaluing everything immediately. This adjustment is real but proportional, and most founders and investors in normal market conditions see it as fair. This is the approach you should aim for.

Board Composition and Governance

Control terms receive less attention than economic terms in most fundraising conversations, and that is a mistake. The board or investor governance structure determines who has authority over the most consequential decisions your company will face.

The story of Steve Jobs's removal from Apple in 1985 is one of the most well-known examples of what happens when a board exercises its authority against a founder's interests. Jobs had co-founded the company, led the development of the Macintosh, and shaped the product vision that defined Apple's early identity. None of that protected him when the board, supported by the investors and the CEO he himself had helped hire, stripped him of his operational role. The board had the legal authority to do it. They exercised it.

Jobs formally left Apple in 1985, and it would be nearly twelve years before he returned. In 1997, he rejoined Apple and helped lead it through a remarkable turnaround, overseeing its rise to become one of the most-valuable companies in the world. The period in between was painful for Jobs and costly for Apple, as the company drifted without a clear, visionary direction.

The lesson isn't that boards always behave badly. It's that the makeup of the board—its incentives, background, and alignment with founders—can profoundly shape what is possible, both positively and negatively. Founding a company does not shield you from your own governance structure if you have relinquished the formal authority that structure controls.

As noted in the chapter outline, not every investment results in a formal board. An angel investing $50,000 through a SAFE is unlikely to take a board seat. An institutional seed fund investing $2 million usually will. By Series A, a formal board with a defined composition is almost always in place.

A typical early-stage board for an institutionally funded company has three to five seats. Founders hold one or two, investors hold one or two, and an independent director is often added as a neutral party. The composition matters because certain decisions require board approval: issuing new equity, making acquisitions, approving the annual budget, and in some cases, hiring or removing senior executives.

A board with a majority of seats held by investors can make decisions that go against the founder's wishes. This usually occurs when the company isn't meeting expectations and the investor believes a change in direction or leadership is needed. When an investor seeks majority control of the board from the first round, they are signalling they want the power to act unilaterally if necessary. Whether you are comfortable with that depends on how much you trust the investor and how willing you are to risk that trust during through difficult periods.

For smaller raises where a formal board is not formed, the same principles apply to the governance rights documented in the investment agreement. Investor consent rights over major decisions, observer rights at management meetings, and information rights all define the real shape of the relationship, regardless of whether a formal board exists.

Protective Provisions

Protective provisions are veto rights granted to preferred shareholders over specific categories of decisions. They are standard in institutional investment agreements and most are reasonable.

Typical protective provisions give investors the right to block: the sale of the company below a certain price, issuance of new shares that would dilute their holdings, changes to the company's constitution that would affect investor rights, and taking on debt above a specified threshold.

These provisions become problematic when drafted so broadly that they give investors a veto over operational decisions that should belong to the founders. Watch out for provisions that require investor consent for any acquisition regardless of size, any new hire above a certain salary, or any change to the business plan. These provisions give investors operational influence that goes well beyond their role as shareholders.

Two specific provisions deserve a brief explanation because they feature in term sheets more frequently than most founders anticipate.

Drag-along rights give investors the right to force all shareholders, including founders and employees, to approve a sale that the investor supports. If the majority investor wants to sell and you don't, drag-along rights mean they may be able to enforce the deal regardless. The scope of these rights — which shareholders are subject to them and what triggers them — is negotiable and should be examined carefully.

Representations and warranties are legal statements you make about the accuracy of information provided during due diligence. They carry real liability. If a representation turns out to be incorrect, even unintentionally, it can give the investor grounds to seek compensation after the deal closes. Your lawyer should review these carefully and push back on any that are unreasonably broad.

When an investor requests protective provisions that go beyond the standard categories, ask what specific scenario they are trying to safeguard against. The answer tells you something important about how they anticipate the relationship to develop.

Red Flags in a Term Sheet

Some terms signal a genuine problem with the proposed relationship. When you encounter the following, stop and think carefully before proceeding.

A participation multiple above 1x. This signals an investor who is focused on downside protection at your expense. It is not the profile of a partner who expects a large and shared outcome.

Full ratchet anti-dilution is uncommon in typical market conditions. An investor insisting on it is likely either inexperienced or anticipating a difficult trajectory.

Investor-controlled board from the first round. Giving majority board control to an investor before the business has proven itself creates a situation that is very difficult to reverse and that limits your authority at the moments you need it most.

Redemption rights. These give an investor the right to demand their money back after a certain period if no liquidity event has occurred. They create a sword hanging over the business that can force a premature sale or a damaging restructuring at the worst possible time. They are rare but not unheard of.

Broad consent rights over operational decisions. If the investor needs to approve hiring decisions, budget changes, or product direction, they are not a financial partner. They are an operating partner with full influence and limited accountability for the consequences.

None of these terms automatically means you should walk away. Sometimes the right investor comes with a term that requires negotiation. But each one is a signal worth taking seriously, and a founder who signs without understanding them is agreeing to conditions they haven't fully considered.

What Is Actually Negotiable

First-time founders often assume that a term sheet is mostly fixed and that negotiating it risks the deal. That belief costs founders their money and control.

Start with the terms that most directly influence your financial outcome and your control. Begin with the liquidation preference structure, as it determines what you receive in the most likely exit scenarios. Next, consider board composition, since it determines who controls the company's most important decisions. Third, review the anti-dilution clause, because it impacts how you're treated if performance falls short. Finally, consider the timing of the option pool, as it's the easiest to model and the simplest to negotiate once the other terms are agreed upon. Everything else is of lesser importance.

What is generally non-negotiable: the existence of a liquidation preference, some form of anti-dilution protection, essential protective provisions on major decisions, and access to information rights. These are fundamental elements of the investor relationship that exist for legitimate reasons on both sides.

The most effective way to negotiate is from knowledge rather than emotion. A founder who says, "I'd like to discuss the participating preference because at a $20 million exit, it reduces founder proceeds by $3 million relative to a non-participating structure", is having a different conversation than a founder who says, "This doesn't feel fair." Know the numbers. Run the scenarios. Make the argument with data.

And get a good lawyer. Not one new to venture transactions, but one who regularly handles deals at your stage and understands what market standard looks like in your specific market. The cost of experienced legal counsel at this stage is minor compared to the value of the terms you protect.

8

Closing the Deal

A signed term sheet might seem like the finish line. It isn't; it's the starting gun for another phase of fundraising that is just as demanding. Many founders aren't prepared for this stage, which often leads to deals collapsing or needing last-minute restructuring.

The period between a signed term sheet and money in the bank typically takes four to eight weeks at seed stage and eight to sixteen weeks at Series A. During that time, the investor is conducting due diligence, the lawyers on both sides are negotiating final documents, and the founder is trying to run the business while managing everything simultaneously. Getting through this period well requires the same deliberate preparation that got you to the term sheet in the first place.

What Due Diligence Actually Involves

Due diligence is the investor's process of verifying that what you told them in the pitch is accurate. It is thorough, sometimes uncomfortable, and entirely legitimate. An investor committing significant capital to a company has an obligation to their own investors to check the claims they're backing.

What gets examined depends on the stage and the investor, but the core areas are consistent.

Financial verification means the investor will want to see your actual accounts, not just the management summary you presented in the pitch. Bank statements, revenue records, payroll records, and any outstanding liabilities will all be reviewed. Any discrepancy between what was presented and what the records show is a serious problem. Small errors in financial presentations are common and usually forgivable if corrected immediately. Patterns of inconsistency or numbers that can't be reconciled are not.

Customer references are standard for most institutional raises. The investor will want to speak directly with two to four of your customers to verify that the relationships are real, that the customers value the product as described, and that the revenue figures are accurate. Prepare your customers for these calls in advance. Brief them on what the investor is likely to ask, make sure they are willing to participate, and choose customers who can clearly articulate the value the product creates for them.

Legal and corporate structure review includes checking your incorporation documents, your cap table, existing investor agreements, any outstanding debts or financial commitments, and your intellectual property ownership. The IP review is especially crucial for technology companies. Investors will want to verify that the company owns the technology it is built on, not the founders personally and not a previous employer. If any of this is unclear, clarify it before due diligence starts.

Team and background checks differ depending on the investor. Some perform formal reference checks on founders and key executives, while others rely on network checks conducted during the evaluation process. Either way, be transparent about your background from the first meeting. Surprises uncovered during due diligence can be damaging, even if the facts are harmless, because discovering something undisclosed raises doubts about what else might be hidden.

Technical review is typical at Series A for software startups, where an investor might hire a technical advisor to evaluate the product's architecture, scalability, and code quality. At seed stage, this is less common but still possible. If your technical infrastructure has known weaknesses, acknowledge them openly and outline your plan to fix them.

The founders who move through due diligence fastest are those who anticipated it. The data room you built in Chapter 4, clean, organised, and complete, becomes your most valuable asset in this phase. An investor who receives everything they ask for promptly, and who finds that the documents match what they were told in the pitch, gains confidence rapidly. An investor who waits days for documents and finds inconsistencies loses it just as fast.

When Deals Fall Apart

Not every process that reaches due diligence closes. Understanding why deals fail at this stage is the most practical preparation you can do.

The most common cause is a material discrepancy, meaning a difference between what was represented in the pitch and what the underlying documents show is significant enough to affect the investment decision. This happens more often than founders expect and more often than investors discuss publicly.

In Australia, several high-profile seed and Series A deals that reached the term sheet stage between 2021 and 2023 fell apart during due diligence when revenue figures shown in pitch materials couldn't be matched with actual bank statements and accounting records.These incidents were covered in the Australian Financial Review and the startup press at the time. In each case, the founders claimed that the discrepancies were due to how revenue was calculated, not deliberate misrepresentation. However, the investors who walked away did not see it that way. The outcome was the same: the deal collapsed, relationships were permanently strained, and the founders' ability to secure funding from other investors within the same ecosystem was significantly impaired.

The lesson is not that investors are unforgiving. It's that a problem disclosed in the pitch is a data point that investors can discuss and evaluate. The same problem discovered in due diligence is a breach of trust that ends the process regardless of the underlying explanation. Tell investors the difficult things early, before they find them.

The second common cause is a change in market conditions or the investor's portfolio during the process. If a fund has committed heavily to new investments in the past month, their appetite for an additional deal may reduce. If a comparable company in their portfolio has hit problems, their thesis on the sector may shift. These causes are outside your control. The response is to manage your own timeline carefully: set a clear deadline for close at the point of signing the term sheet and hold the investor to it professionally.

The third cause is founder behaviour during due diligence. Slow responses, evasiveness, or signs of disorganisation that undermine the confidence the pitch created. This one is entirely within your control. Treat the due diligence period as an extension of the pitch. The investor is still forming their view of you. The quality of your responses, the speed of your turnarounds, and the consistency between what you said and what the documents show are all data points they are using to calibrate how much confidence to place in your judgment.

The Legal Documents

Once due diligence is largely finished, the lawyers start drafting the final investment documents. Before explaining what those documents include, it's worth understanding what each one does in the deal, because the purpose of each shapes what you should focus on when reviewing it.

For a priced equity round, three documents form the core of the close. The shareholders' agreement governs the ongoing relationship between all shareholders. It is the document that gives legal form to the term sheet, translating the economic and control provisions negotiated earlier into binding legal obligations. This is the document that deserves your most careful reading.

The subscription agreement is the contract under which the investor actually pays their money in exchange for shares. It is more mechanical than the shareholders' agreement but contains your representations and warranties, the legal statements you are making about the accuracy of information provided during the process, which carry real liability if they turn out to be incorrect. The updated constitutional documents, called articles of association in Australia and the UK or a certificate of incorporation in the US, reflect any changes to the company's formal structure required by the new investment. Of these three, the shareholders' agreement is the one to prioritise.

For a convertible note or SAFE, the documentation is simpler, which is one of the reasons those instruments dominate at seed stage.

A seed round data room at close typically covers four areas. Your corporate structure: incorporation documents and a current cap table showing all shares including options and any convertible instruments. Your financial history: statements for the past two years, if available, plus monthly management accounts for the current year. Your customer evidence: contracts or anonymised data showing the relationships described in the pitch. And your intellectual property: any registrations or pending applications covering the core technology.

Read the shareholders' agreement yourself before your lawyer summarises it. The summary will be accurate, but reading the actual document is the only way to understand the full scope of what you're agreeing to.

Common points of renegotiation at this stage include the specific wording of consent rights, the definition of what constitutes a liquidity event, the scope of founder representations and warranties, and the details of any restrictive covenants on the founders. None of these should be entirely new issues at this stage, since the term sheet should have indicated the investor's position on the major items. But lawyers on both sides will push on the edges of each clause, and some renegotiation is normal.

Where it is not normal, and where you should pay close attention is if an investor's lawyers introduce new provisions in the final documents that were not included in the term sheet. Report this immediately and directly to the investor, not through lawyers. Occasionally, new provisions that appear after signing the term sheet may be due to a genuine oversight. However, they can also sometimes indicate a deliberate attempt to amend terms after the founder has committed. Do not overlook this.

Managing Multiple Closing Parties

Seed rounds often involve several investors: a lead investor who determines the terms and one or more smaller investors participating on the same or similar terms. Managing the close across multiple parties adds complexity that founders consistently underestimate.

Each investor has their own lawyer, their own review timeline, and their own questions. The lead investor's documents typically set the template, and smaller investors are usually asked to sign the same agreement with minimal changes. But smaller investors sometimes request amendments, and those requests need to be managed carefully. An amendment that benefits one investor may have implications for others, and changes that seem minor can reopen negotiations that were considered settled.

A staggered close, where different investors sign and fund at different times rather than all on the same date, introduces specific risks. Early investors are committed while later investors can still withdraw, creating a period of uncertainty about whether the full round will be completed. Where possible, aim for a simultaneous close with all parties signing on the same day. If a staggered close is unavoidable, set a firm deadline for all parties and communicate it clearly from the beginning.

Appoint yourself as the single point of contact for all investor communications during the close, with support from your lawyer. Fragmented communication across multiple parties is a reliable source of confusion and delay. Keep all investors informed of the overall timeline, flag any issues promptly, and maintain the momentum that got you to this point.

The Legal Documents and Venture Debt

Some founders use the close of an equity round as a chance to add venture debt, which are loans usually backed by the company's assets or future equity, to extend the runway between rounds.

Venture debt is becoming more common and can be a valuable tool for founders who want additional capital without additional dilution. But it comes with a specific risk that equity does not: financial covenants. A covenant is a condition attached to the loan that the borrower must meet on an ongoing basis. Common covenants require the company to keep a minimum cash balance, avoid taking on more debt without the lender's approval, or achieve certain revenue targets. If a covenant is breached, the lender can demand immediate full repayment of the loan. This is not a minor issue. A breach of covenant at a tough moment for the business can turn a cash flow problem into an existential crisis.

Founders should understand exactly what covenants they are agreeing to before signing a venture debt facility, model what happens to the business if those covenants are breached, and ensure their lawyer reviews the terms as carefully as the equity documents.

The First 90 Days After Close

The capital is in the bank. The process is over. Now the real work starts, and the patterns established in the first 90 days will define the investor relationship for everything that follows.

Setting up governance correctly is the first priority. Whether your arrangement involves a formal board, a defined investor group, or a more informal structure, document it clearly and get it operating from the start. If a board is being formed, schedule the first meeting within 30 days of close and run it properly. Send a clear agenda and a pre-read pack at least five business days in advance. Record decisions in minutes. If the arrangement is less formal, agree on the communication cadence in writing before the close has even settled. Investors who find themselves three months post-close with no agreed structure and no clear communication rhythm become anxious investors. Anxious investors create problems that structure would have prevented.

Establishing your reporting rhythm is the second priority and the one most directly connected to how your investors behave when things get difficult. Decide what you will send, how often, and in what format, and then deliver it without fail. A monthly investor update that arrives on the same date each month, covers the key metrics honestly, takes no more than ten minutes to read, and includes both what is going well and what is not, is one of the most effective relationship-management tools a founder has. Investors who feel informed stay patient. Investors who feel uninformed start asking questions at the wrong moments and in the wrong forums.

A good monthly update covers revenue and key metrics versus the targets committed to at close, the two or three most significant things that happened in the past month, the most important focus areas for the month ahead, any places where investor help would be useful, and any material risks the investor should be aware of. That last item is the one founders most consistently omit, and it is the most important. An investor who learns about a problem in a monthly update is almost always more helpful than one who discovers the same problem has been developing for months while the updates showed everything as fine.

Communicating your capital deployment plan is the third priority. Before you spend a significant portion of what you've raised, share with your investors how you plan to deploy it and which milestones you aim to achieve. This is not asking for permission. It is demonstrating that you have a disciplined plan for the funds they have entrusted to you. Outline the specific milestones the capital is intended to reach, the assumptions behind those targets, and how you'll determine if you're on or off track. Investors who see a clear deployment plan aligned with defined milestones tend to be confident. Meanwhile, investors who see money leaving the account without a clear framework get nervous, and nervous investors are more difficult to manage than confident ones.

A Real Example of a Clean Close

When Airwallex, the Australian financial technology company, closed its Series B round in 2018, the founders had prepared extensively for the process. The due diligence was completed faster than the investors expected, because the financial records were clean, the cap table was clear, and the legal documents were in order. The round, led by Tencent and Sequoia Capital China, was completed in a remarkably short time, which is fast for a round of that size.

The founders attributed the speed partly to the quality of their data-room preparation and partly to the transparency of their communications throughout the process. Nothing uncovered in due diligence contradicted anything said in the pitch. That consistency told the investors something important about how the founders operated, and it established a tone that carried forward into every subsequent raise.

Airwallex went on to raise over $900 million in subsequent rounds, reaching a valuation of around $5.5 billion. The smooth, well-executed early close was not incidental to that trajectory. It helped establish the credibility and trust that underpinned the company's later growth.

The close isn't the end of your relationship with investors; it's the start. Chapter 9 explores what that relationship looks like throughout its full lifecycle, including the tough moments every company will face.

9

Managing Your Investors

Every book about raising capital ends when the money arrives. This one doesn't, because the moment the capital lands is the moment the most important and least discussed part of the whole experience begins.

The investor relationship is long. A seed investor who backs you today may still be on your cap table in eight years. A Series A investor will be involved in every major decision your company makes for the next five to seven years at the very least. That is a longer working relationship than most people have with any single colleague, and it carries more consequence than almost any other professional relationship you will have as a founder.

Most founders handle communication reactively. They send updates when things are going well, go quiet when things are hard, and mainly engage with investors primarily when they need something. This is the single most common and most damaging mistake founders make in the post-funding phase. It undermines trust exactly when it matters most and influences how investors behave during the company's inevitable difficult periods.

This chapter covers how to manage the investor relationship proactively, professionally, and honestly throughout the entire investment lifecycle, including the aspects nobody likes to talk about.

The Nature of the Relationship

Understanding what the investor relationship truly is helps you manage it effectively. It's not a friendship, though it may develop some elements of one over time. It's not an employment relationship, even if investors sometimes behave as if it is. It's a formal partnership between parties with partly aligned and partly divergent interests, governed by legal documents, sustained by trust, and made complex by the fact that both of these factors are present at the same time.

The aligned interests are real. Your investors want the company to succeed. Their financial return depends entirely on your success, which means they are genuinely motivated to help when they can. That motivation is not unconditional, but it is genuine.

The divergent interests are equally real. Your investors have a defined fund timeline that may not match your vision. They have a portfolio of other companies competing for their attention. And in difficult situations their obligation, their fiduciary duty meaning their legal responsibility to act in the interests of their own investors first, means protecting the fund's return, not necessarily protecting your equity or your continued role. Pretending otherwise doesn't change it. Understanding it does.

Neither of these realities makes the relationship bad. They make it human, and, like all human relationships, it is best managed when it is managed honestly.

Setting Up for Success From Day One

The patterns established in the first 90 days after close, covered at the end of Chapter 8, matter more than most founders realise. But the underlying principle extends well beyond those first three months. What you do consistently, from the first investor update to the last meeting before an exit, is what defines the relationship.

The most important thing you can do consistently is communicate proactively and honestly. Not just when things are good. Not just when you need something. All the time, on a predictable cadence, with enough substance that the investor genuinely understands how the business is tracking.

This sounds obvious. It is not common.

Founders who do this well create a distinct dynamic with their investors. Because the investor is never surprised, they are never anxious. Because they are never anxious, they are collaborative rather than interventionist. Because they are collaborative, they are genuinely useful when the founder needs help. The founders who communicate poorly create the opposite dynamic. Investors who don't know what is happening fill the gap with assumptions, and assumptions in the absence of information are rarely optimistic. They become more demanding. They raise topics in board or investor meetings that the founder would have preferred to address privately. All of this is avoidable with a well-written monthly update.

The Monthly Investor Update

The monthly investor update is one of the most effective relationship management tools available to a founder, and it takes less than two hours a month to do it well.

Stewart Butterfield has spoken about the discipline this required during the early days of Slack. Slack began as an internal communication tool for a gaming company called Glitch. When Glitch failed around 2012, the team pivoted to develop Slack as a standalone product.

During that transition, when the outcome was genuinely uncertain and the evidence was limited, Butterfield maintained a consistent communication rhythm with his investors. He was honest about what wasn't working, specific about what the team was learning, and clear about what they were trying next. In multiple interviews, he has cited this kind of disciplined, transparent communication as central to maintaining investor confidence during a period when the conventional signal—a working product with paying customers—simply wasn't there yet.

Slack launched publicly in 2013 and grew to over 10 million daily active users within five years. The investor relationships that endured through the uncertain period were those built on consistent, honest communication during it.

A good monthly update is not a press release. It is an honest, concise account of where the business stands, written for people who care deeply about the outcome and have a legitimate interest in knowing the truth. It should take the investor no more than ten minutes to read and should leave them with a clear picture of momentum, challenges, and what comes next.

The structure that works consistently covers six areas. Revenue and key metrics, the specific numbers relevant to your business model and growth stage, reported against whatever targets were agreed at close or in the previous update. The two or three most significant things that happened in the past month, good or bad. The two or three things the team is most focused on in the coming month. Any places where an investor can help, an introduction, a reference, or a piece of advice would be genuinely useful. Any material risks or problems the investor should be aware of. And a brief cash position update showing runway.

That last item, the honest reporting of problems and risks, is the one founders most consistently omit. It is the most important. Investors who learn about a serious problem in a monthly update are almost always more helpful and more measured in their response than investors who hear about the same problem when it has become a crisis. The investor who finds out at a quarterly meeting that revenue has been declining for three months while the monthly updates showed everything was fine is not just disappointed by the business performance. They are disturbed by the founder's judgment and honesty. That is a much harder thing to recover from than the revenue decline itself.

Running Effective Governance Meetings

Whether your investor arrangement involves a formal board or a more informal investor group, the meeting structure deserves the same attention.

A formal board meeting should run for two to three hours and cover the business in sufficient depth that the board can make informed decisions on matters requiring its approval. The agenda should be sent with a pre-read pack at least five business days in advance. The pre-read should include the monthly metrics, a management report covering the key themes in the business, any decisions requiring board approval, and any items the founder wants to discuss. Board members who arrive prepared because the pre-read was thorough and timely are a fundamentally different group to work with than board members who are reading materials for the first time in the meeting itself.

For a less formal investor group, the same principles apply with adjusted mechanics. A quarterly call with a shared document summarising business performance, a clear agenda, and time for genuine discussion is better than an ad hoc call triggered by a problem.

Run the meeting rather than letting it run you. Come prepared with a clear view of what you want to discuss, the decisions you need, and what you want investors to take away from the time together. Founders who chair their own investor meetings confidently, guiding discussion, managing time, and finalising decisions, send an important message about how they run their company. After each meeting, send a brief summary of what was discussed, the decisions made, and the action items. This prevents confusion that can arise three weeks later when two people remember a decision differently.

Using Investors as a Resource

Most founders underuse their investors, particularly in the early months when they are still figuring out the relationship. Investors who have backed multiple companies in your sector have seen patterns you haven't encountered yet. They have networks you don't have access to. They have made mistakes building and backing companies, and many will share what they learned if you ask directly.

The key is specificity. Asking an investor for "any introductions that might be useful" produces little. Asking an investor to introduce you to the head of enterprise sales at a specific company in their portfolio, because you are trying to understand how they structured their sales team at 50 people, produces a useful conversation. Investors respond to specific, well-framed requests from founders who have clearly thought about what they need.

Some investors are significantly more useful than others, and part of managing the relationship well is understanding where each investor's genuine value lies. An investor with deep sector experience is worth asking about market dynamics. An investor with a strong operator background is worth asking about team structure. An investor with a wide network of later-stage funds is worth involving when you start thinking about the next raise. Play to what each investor is actually good at rather than treating them as interchangeable.

When Things Go Wrong

The instinct is to hold back. The company is missing its targets. A key person has resigned. A competitor has launched something that poses a threat. And the founder's initial reaction is to wait until there's something better to report before informing the investors.

That instinct is almost always the wrong call, and it is the one that most damages the relationship.

Ben Horowitz has documented his approach to this in *The Hard Thing About Hard Things* with a specificity that most business books avoid. During Loudcloud's most difficult periods, including a near-death experience when the company was burning through cash and publicly traded with a collapsing stock price, Horowitz did not wait for good news before talking to his board. He told them what was happening as it was happening, including the parts where he didn't yet know what to do. His account describes board members who responded to that transparency by becoming more actively helpful, not more demanding or more critical.

One board member helped him identify a potential acquirer for a part of the business, and that connection led directly to the sale of Loudcloud's cloud-services business to EDS for 63.5 million dollars in cash, a deal that stabilised the company's finances and gave it the runway to pivot to Opsware. That board meeting only happened because Horowitz had been honest about how serious the situation was. If he had managed the news carefully rather than shared it candidly, the connection — and that crucial lifeline — would never have been made.

The principle holds at every scale. Tell your investors when something material changes, even if you don't yet know what you'll do about it. A brief note that says "our largest customer has indicated they may not renew, which represents 20 percent of our revenue. We are meeting with them next week and will know more shortly. I wanted you to know immediately" is exactly the right response. It is honest, timely, and treats the investor as a partner rather than an audience to be managed. Then follow up with what you learn, and then with what you're doing about it. Investors who are kept in the loop during a crisis step up to help. Investors who feel excluded from a crisis focus on protecting their position.

Navigating Investor Pressure

There will be moments when your investors want something you don't. A pivot you don't believe in. A hire you think is wrong. A sale of the company that you want to resist. A change in strategy that conflicts with your vision.

The first and most important thing to understand is the difference between investor pressure as a conversation and investor pressure as a governance event. These require different responses.

When an investor expresses a view, recommends a course of action, or pushes for a change during a meeting or a call, that constitutes a conversation. You are not required to agree. You must listen attentively, engage sincerely, and explain your reasoning clearly. Investors who feel heard and understood, even if they are overruled, stay collaborative. Investors who feel dismissed or ignored become difficult. The response to investor pressure should be conversation, not compliance or avoidance.

When an investor exercises legal authority through a board vote, a consent right, or a protective provision documented in the shareholders' agreement, that is a governance event. The rules are different. What they can do depends entirely on the terms you signed. If you maintained a founder-controlled board or an evenly balanced governance structure, you have real authority over most operational decisions. If you gave investors majority control early, your options are more constrained. This is one of the reasons board composition matters so much at the term sheet stage. The terms you negotiate determine your options in the difficult moments.

The founders who handle investor pressure most effectively are those who disagree by engaging, not by withdrawing. They present data. They communicate their own analysis clearly. They recognise the investor's concerns as legitimate, even when they reach a different conclusion. And they make decisions transparently so the investor understands the reasoning, even if they don't agree.

What you should avoid is the gradual erosion of the relationship through avoidance. Founders who stop returning calls, cancel investor meetings, send vague updates when specific ones are expected, and make decisions without communication create the conditions for investor escalation. An investor who feels ignored begins looking at the legal documents to understand their options. An investor who feels included and respected remains engaged in the conversation.

Reputation Is a Long Asset

How you behave under investor pressure, how you communicate when things are hard, and whether you follow through on your commitments all shape your reputation within a community that is smaller and more interconnected than it appears from the outside.

The startup investing community in any major market consists of hundreds of active investors, not thousands. They know each other well. They co-invest. They share notes informally on founders they've met and companies they've seen. The Series A investor who is considering your company will contact your seed investors before they call you. They will ask three questions: Did this founder communicate honestly when things were tough? Did they do what they said they would do? And would you back them again?

Those three answers carry more weight in that conversation than your pitch deck. They are shaped entirely by how you managed the relationship over the preceding eighteen months.

Reid Hoffman has written and spoken about this dynamic extensively in *Blitzscaling* and across his *Masters of Scale* content. His framework for thinking about reputation in professional networks is directly applicable here: reputation is not built in the moments when everything is working. It is built in the moments when it would be easier to be less than honest, to avoid a difficult conversation, or to prioritise short-term comfort over long-term trust. Those are the moments investors remember, and those are the moments that determine what they say when someone calls to ask about you.

Founders who raise their Series A quickly and on strong terms are almost always supported by enthusiastic seed investors. Those who struggle to secure a follow-on round, even with good business performance, may face reservations from someone who has seen them up close and shared their concerns privately.

Your investor relationships are a long-term asset. Manage them accordingly. The Series A investor evaluating your company will call your seed investors before they call you. They will ask whether you communicated honestly when things were hard, whether you did what you said you would do, and whether they would back you again. Those three answers carry more weight than your pitch deck. They are built or damaged every month, in every update you send, in every difficult conversation you have or avoid.

10

Setting Up for the Next Raise

The moment the capital from your current raise is in the bank, the countdown for the next one begins. Not because you should be thinking about raising funds when your focus should be on building, but because the decisions you make today with this capital will shape whether you will have options in twelve to eighteen months, or whether you'll be forced to raise funds out of desperation.

Capital Is a Tool, Not an Outcome

Founders who have just closed a round often feel, briefly, that the toughest part is behind them. The fundraising was draining, the negotiations were stressful, and having the capital in the account feels like solid ground after months of uncertainty. That feeling is genuine, and you've earned it.

It passes quickly.

Start with the milestone. Not the budget, not the headcount plan, not the product roadmap. Focus on the milestone. The capital you raised was sized, either explicitly or implicitly, to get the company from its current position toward a specific stage of development. At seed stage, this is often when you can show enough evidence to secure a Series A. At Series A, it's usually the point where the business can maintain its growth path without needing additional equity funding, or where it's ready to pursue a growth round.

If you can't state that milestone in one sentence, you'll waste the capital without a clear plan. And capital spent without a plan won't secure the next raise.

Before you spend a significant portion of what you've raised, write down the answers to three questions. What milestone does this capital need to get the company to? What does achieving that milestone enable that isn't possible now? And what is the single biggest risk to reaching it? These three questions won't take long to answer. The discipline of writing them down before spending begins is what separates founders who deploy capital wisely from those who look up twelve months later and wonder where it went.

What the Next Stage Requires

The gap between seed stage and Series A is where many well-funded startups quietly stall. The seed investors are patient, the product is improving, the team is growing, and the founder assumes the momentum is sufficient. Then Series A conversations begin, and the founders discover that what they've built, while real progress, doesn't yet meet the bar.

Canva's transition from its early seed funding to institutional backing is one of the most-studied in Australian startup history, and it illustrates this point directly. Melanie Perkins did not deploy Canva's early seed capital—around $3 million raised in 2013—against a general sense of growth. Instead, she used it to hit specific milestones: user numbers that would demonstrate genuine demand, a product experience that would retain those users, and evidence of international traction that would make the scale of the opportunity credible to a global investor.

When Matrix Partners and later funds led Canva's first significant institutional rounds, the evidence Perkins presented had been deliberately built over the preceding period, not left to chance. Canva went on to raise over $500 million in subsequent rounds and reach a valuation of around $40 billion. The discipline of the early capital deployment was the foundation of everything that followed.

The seed to Series A transition is primarily a revenue story. Series A investors want to see annual recurring revenue of between $1 million and $3 million in most markets, growing at a rate that implies meaningful scale within two to three years. The specific number is less important than the trajectory and the quality of the revenue: low churn, growing customer value, and a customer acquisition process that doesn't require the founder personally closing every deal.

If you raised seed capital and your current annual recurring revenue is $300,000, you can work backwards from a $1.5 million target to understand what growth rate you need to sustain and for how long. That calculation tells you how to weight your capital deployment between product development, sales, and marketing. It also tells you roughly when you will be ready to raise again.

The Series A to Series B transition is primarily a scale story. Series B investors want to see that the business model works at volume: that the unit economics hold as you grow, that the organisation can execute without the founder's direct involvement in every function, and that the market opportunity is larger than what the Series A thesis assumed. Revenue at this stage is typically between $5 million and $20 million annually, and the growth rate matters more than the absolute number.

Each transition has its own specific proof points, and the capital you have today is the fuel required to reach them. Spend it with that destination in mind.

The Metrics That Drive the Next Conversation

Not all metrics are created equal at a fundraising conversation. Some tell a story that investors respond to. Others describe activity without revealing whether the business model actually works.

At the seed-to-Series-A transition, two metrics matter more than all others.

Monthly recurring revenue growth over a sustained period, twelve months or more, is the single most powerful number in a growth-stage pitch. A single good month followed by flatness is not a growth story. Twelve months of consistent growth is. This is the metric that tells an investor whether the trajectory is real, and it is the one that is hardest to manufacture because it requires sustained execution rather than a single well-timed effort.

Net revenue retention, meaning whether existing customers are spending more or less over time, tells an investor about the quality of the product and the depth of customer relationships. A rate above 100 percent means existing customers are expanding their spend faster than others are churning, which is a powerful signal of product-market fit at scale. This is the metric most seed-stage founders fail to track early enough. Start tracking it from your first cohort of customers, meaning the first group of customers who joined in the same period, so that by the time you reach a Series A conversation you have real data rather than a recent calculation.

Supporting these two are the metrics covered in Chapter 4: customer acquisition cost, customer lifetime value, and gross margin. At the seed-to-Series-A transition, investors want to see these moving in the right direction. At Series A to Series B, they want to see them proven at scale, demonstrated across multiple cohorts over multiple periods rather than estimated from limited early data.

Track all of these metrics monthly. Build a dashboard that shows the trends clearly. The founders who walk into a Series A meeting and can show eighteen months of clean, consistently tracked data are at a significant advantage over those reconstructing figures from partial records.

When to Start the Next Process

Most founders start the next raise too late. The pattern is consistent and the cause is understandable. The business demands full attention, the current investors are supportive, and the runway feels comfortable until suddenly it doesn't. By the time the founder starts serious investor conversations, there are four months of runway left and the entire dynamic of the raise has changed.

Start the next process when you have twelve to fifteen months of runway remaining. Not when you have six. Not when the board suggests it's time. Twelve to fifteen months.

This timeline matters for several reasons. It gives you enough runway to run the process properly, including due diligence and legal close, without the pressure of an imminent crisis. It gives you the option to walk away from a term sheet that doesn't meet your standards and start again. It means you are raising from strength, because the business is operating normally and you are choosing to grow rather than raising from necessity because the alternative is closing.

The relationship-building for the next raise should begin earlier still. Twelve to eighteen months before you plan to formally raise, start having conversations with the investors you want to target. Not pitching. Updating them on the business, sharing what you're learning, asking for their perspective on the market. By the time you formally start the process, these investors already know the company, have watched it develop over time, and have formed a positive impression before your first formal pitch meeting. This is exactly what your current investors did when they first met you, whether you realised it at the time or not.

Your Current Investors Are Your Strongest Asset in the Next Raise

A founder raising a Series A from investors who don't know them is at a significant disadvantage compared to a founder whose seed investors are active advocates. The best thing you can do for the next raise, starting today, is manage the current investor relationship so well that those investors become enthusiastic supporters of the next process.

Seed investors who have been kept informed, respected, and engaged are typically willing to do several things in a subsequent raise. They will make direct introductions to Series A funds they know. They will take reference calls from interested investors and speak specifically and positively about the founder's communication, judgment, and execution under pressure. They will, in many cases, participate in the next round themselves, which creates a powerful signal of insider confidence that outside investors pay close attention to.

None of this happens automatically. It is the product of eighteen months or more of consistent, honest, professional management of the relationship. The investor who has received a clear monthly update every month, who has been told about problems before they became crises, and who has seen the founder make and explain good decisions under difficult conditions, is an investor who will advocate strongly when the time comes. Chapter 9 covered how to build that relationship. This is the return on that investment.

The Question You Need to Answer

There is a question that sits underneath every chapter in this book, and the right place to address it directly is here, near the end, when you have enough context to answer it well.

What do you actually want?

Not what you're supposed to want. Not what the startup culture around you celebrates. Not what your investors want, or what the founders you admire have built. What do you actually want from this company over the next ten years, and what does a good personal outcome look like for you?

Write the answer down in one sentence. If you can't write it in one sentence, you haven't answered it yet. "I want to build a large company" is not an answer. "I want to build a company I can run for twenty years and eventually pass on" is an answer. "I want to generate a return that gives my family financial security within ten years" is an answer. Both are legitimate. Both lead to different decisions at every significant fork in the road, from which investors to take, to what terms to accept, to how hard to push for control at each raise, to when to consider selling.

Share the answer with your co-founder if you have one. Check whether your answer and theirs are compatible. If they aren't, that incompatibility will surface eventually, and the earlier you find it the less damage it does. Then revisit the question every year, because the answer changes as the company changes and as you change.

The research on this is consistent. Founders who are explicit about their goals from the beginning make more coherent decisions, experience less conflict with investors and co-founders, and report higher satisfaction with their outcomes regardless of the financial result. Not because having a clear goal guarantees success, but because it means the path you chose was the one you actually wanted to be on.

This question has been sitting quietly underneath every chapter in this book. Whether to raise, from whom, on what terms, how to manage the relationship, when to start the next process: all of these decisions look different depending on the answer. You now have enough context to answer it honestly. The next step is yours.

CONCLUSION
The Founder Who Raises Smart

Most founders who struggle with funding don't struggle because their business isn't good enough. They struggle because they walked into the process without understanding what they were actually doing.

This book has been about changing that. Not by making funding feel simpler than it is, but by giving you the understanding to make every decision in the process consciously rather than by default.

The Insights That Matter Most

Five ideas run through this book that are worth carrying with you beyond it.

Funding is a choice, not a reflex. The decision of whether to raise, and which type of capital to take, is the most consequential decision in the funding journey and the one most founders make by default. The alternative paths are real. The trade-offs are specific. A founder who chooses equity capital after genuinely considering the alternatives is in a fundamentally different position than one who raises because it seemed like the obvious next step.

The terms matter more than the valuation. Founders who spend their negotiating energy on headline valuation while agreeing to participating liquidation preferences, investor-controlled boards, and punitive anti-dilution provisions have optimised the wrong variable. A lower valuation with clean terms will almost always produce a better outcome than a higher valuation with aggressive provisions. Know what you're signing before you sign it.

Investors are partners with a different agenda. The investor relationship is genuinely collaborative and genuinely adversarial at the same time. Understanding both dimensions, rather than defaulting to the partnership framing that most fundraising advice promotes, is what allows a founder to manage the relationship honestly and protect their own interests without damaging the trust that makes the relationship work.

Communication is the job. The founders who build the best investor relationships are not distinguished by the quality of their businesses. They are distinguished by the quality of their communication: consistent, honest, and specific, including when the news is bad. That discipline is what converts investors from capital providers into advocates. It is also what builds the reputation that opens doors in every subsequent raise.

The process is the preparation. Every rejected pitch, every tough due diligence question, and investor who passes with useful feedback is part of that preparation for the conversation that leads to a closing. Founders who raise funds most efficiently are almost always those who view early rejections as data points rather than final verdicts.

What Comes Next

Picture the founder who has applied what this book covers. They have made a conscious decision about whether and how to raise. They have prepared the evidence before the first meeting rather than during it. They have chosen investors whose interests align with their own, negotiated terms they understand, and closed a deal that reflects genuine strength rather than desperation.

After the close, they set up their governance structure on day one. They send monthly updates that investors actually read. They tell investors about problems early, before they turn into crises. They build relationships that create enthusiastic advocates instead of anxious shareholders.

When the time comes to raise funds again, they don't scramble. They have been building the next raise for twelve months. Their current investors are already making calls on their behalf. The process runs faster, on better terms, with less damage to the business in the meantime.

That outcome is not reserved for exceptional founders with exceptional businesses. It is available to any founder who treats the funding process as seriously as they treat the product.

The Obstacles You Will Face

Knowing what to do and doing it are different things. Three barriers consistently stand between founders and the outcomes described in this book.

Optimism bias. Founders believe their business is further along than the evidence this isshows, that investors will see what they see, and that the raise will take less time than it does. The antidote is the readiness checklist in Chapter 1 and the honest answers it requires. Apply it before every raise, not after the first meetings have gone badly.

The urgency trap. Most founders raise funds too late, with too little runway, and from a position of need rather than strength. A simple rule to avoid that: start the process when it feels a bit too early. Twelve months of runway is the minimum; fifteen months is better. Relationships with the next round's investors should begin before you actually need their money.

Avoiding tough conversations. With investors, with co-founders, and yourselves. The most damaging decisions during funding are usually the ones that were never explicitly made: the term that wasn't negotiated, the update that wasn't sent when the news was bad, the question about what you truly want that was postponed until the answer was forced upon you. The solution is the discipline to have those conversations early, before the cost of avoiding them compounds.

Your Path Forward

Three steps will take you from reading this book to putting it into practice.

Go back to the chapter most relevant to where you are right now and work through it with your specific situation in mind. Not as a reader absorbing information but as a founder making decisions.

Find one investor relationship to invest in before you need it. Not a pitch. A conversation. Ask for perspective, share what you're building, and treat them as someone whose view you value. Do this consistently over the next twelve months.

Answer the question from Chapter 10. Write it down in one sentence. Share it with your co-founder. Let it inform the next decision you make about capital.

The Final Thought

There is a version of the funding journey that most founders experience: reactive, stressful, and shaped more by circumstance than by choice. They raise when they have to, from whoever will fund them, on terms they didn't fully understand, and spend the next several years managing the consequences.

There is another version. It belongs to the founders who understood that every decision in the funding journey, whether to raise, from whom, on what terms, and what to do with the relationship afterwards, was a choice they could make deliberately.

Those founders don't always create the biggest companies. They don't always secure the best terms. But they build businesses that genuinely reflect what they aimed to achieve, with investors who understood what they were supporting, on terms that offered everyone a fair shot at a good outcome.

That is what raising smart looks like. The knowledge is in this book. The decisions are yours.

PRAISE FOR **MURRAY LONGE**

"Murray distils decades of experience and complex concepts into an accessible roadmap."

KERI A. CLARKE - Start-up industry professional

"Murray has a deep understanding of what he is discussing."

KROL- Amazon Reviewer

PRAISE FOR **MURRAY LONGE'S OTHER BOOKS**

"Like sitting down for an in-depth chat with a knowledgeable, experienced friend in the business. Practical advice based on real world practical success. The writing style makes it easy to read and absorb what might otherwise be quite complex ideas."

WORDSMITH - Amazon Reviewer

"A concise and practical guide for entrepreneurs, packed with clear insights, case studies, and actionable steps. An invaluable resource."

KERI A. CLARKE

"This book is a very well-written, thorough look at every aspect of starting a business. I highly recommend it, especially as it's written by a successful entrepreneur, someone who has actually been through the start-up process from start to finish."

PETER G. - Amazon Reviewer

Made in the USA
Monee, IL
04 November 2026

67380400R00056